UPLAND BIRD
HUNTING

© 1993 by National Rifle Association of America

All rights reserved. Printed in the United States of America. No part of this book may be reproduced in whole or part without written permission.

Produced by the NRA Hunter Services Division. For information on the Hunter Skills Series, NRA Hunter Clinic Program, or becoming a volunteer hunter clinic instructor, contact the National Rifle Association of America, Hunter Services Division, 1600 Rhode Island Avenue NW, Washington, D.C. 20036-3268. Telephone (202) 828-6259.

Library of Congress Catalog Card Number;
92-064159

Main entry under title:
Upland Bird Hunting—NRA Hunter Skills Series

ISBN 0-935998-92-6

HS5N5476 (paperback)   HS5N5501 (hard bound)

ACKNOWLEDGEMENTS

Author
Michael Hanback, Field Editor, *Outdoor Life* and former Managing Editor, *American Hunter,* NRA Publications Division

Editors
Michael Hanback, Field Editor, *Outdoor Life* and former Managing Editor, *American Hunter,* NRA Publications Division
Doug Pifer, Assistant Manager, Materials Development and Production, NRA Hunter Services Division
Bob Belford, Program Specialist, NRA Hunter Skills Education and Development Department

Production Manager
Earl W. Hower, Manager, Materials Development and Production, NRA Hunter Services Division

Illustrator
Doug Pifer, Assistant Manager, Materials Development and Production, NRA Hunter Services Division

Co-Authors and Review Committee
Richard L. DeChambeau, Director, NRA Hunter Services Division
Robert L. Davis, Jr., Manager, NRA Youth Hunting Skills and Schools Department
Gary Kania, Manager, NRA Wildlife Management Department
G. Lee Stinnett, Manager, NRA Hunter Skills Education and Development Department
Phil Johnston, Resource Specialist, NRA Hunter Services Division
Sandy M. Sexton, Editorial Assistant, NRA Materials Development and Production, NRA Hunter Services Division
E. J. Wentworth, Field Representative, NRA Field Services Division, and former Wildlife Biologist — Upland Birds, Georgia Department of Natural Resources
Dan Poole, former President, Wildlife Management Institute, and past Member, NRA Board of Directors, and Hunting and Wildlife Conservation Committee

Kitty Beuchert, Assistant Director, NRA Women's Issues and Information Division and former Program Manager, NRA Hunter Information Department

John M. Mullin, Information Officer, North American Gamebird Association

Russell Sewell, Director of Program Development, Pheasants Forever, Inc.

Jerry Allen, Administrative Vice President and Director of National Operations, Quail Unlimited, Inc.

Ron Burkert, Associate Executive Director of Development, The Ruffed Grouse Society

Bill Goudy, Regional Representative, The Ruffed Grouse Society

Paul Carson, Director of Information and Education, The Ruffed Grouse Society

Clifton A. Hatch, Instructional Design and Educational Consultant, Hatch Communications

The National Rifle Association of America is grateful for the contributions made by the preceding persons, by the North American Gamebird Association, Wildlife Management Institute and the government agencies and organizations credited throughout this book.

Photo Credits

Front Cover Photo by **Joe Workosky**
Back Cover Photo by **Charles J. Farmer**

Caution: Procedures and techniques outlined in this publication may require special abilities, technical knowledge, or safety considerations. The National Rifle Association of America, its agents, officers, and employees accept no responsibility for the results obtained by persons using these procedures and techniques and disclaim all liability for any consequential injuries or damages.

Mention of products or technical data does not necessarily mean they have been tested by the authors or NRA staff, and does not constitute endorsement or verification by the NRA.

Local restrictions may apply to some techniques, procedures, and products in your area. Check local laws and game regulations before proceeding.

NRA Hunter's Code of Ethics

I will consider myself an invited guest of the landowner, seeking his permission, and conduct myself that I may be welcome in the future.

I will obey the rules of safe gun handling and will courteously but firmly insist that others who hunt with me do the same.

I will obey all game laws and regulations, and will insist that my companions do likewise.

I will do my best to acquire marksmanship and hunting skills that assure clean, sportsmanlike kills.

I will support conservation efforts that assure good hunting for future generations of Americans.

I will pass along to younger hunters the attitudes and skills essential to a true outdoor sportsman.

NRA Gun Safety Rules

The fundamental NRA rules for safe gun handling are:

- Always keep the gun pointed in a safe direction.
- Always keep your finger off the trigger until ready to shoot.
- Always keep the gun unloaded until ready to use.

When using or storing a gun always follow these rules:

- Be sure the gun is safe to operate.
- Know how to safely use the gun.
- Use only the correct ammunition for your gun.
- Know your target and what is beyond.
- Wear eye and ear protection as appropriate.
- Never use alcohol or drugs before or while shooting.
- Store guns so they are not accessible to unauthorized persons.

Be aware that certain types of guns and many shooting activities require additional safety precautions.

To learn more about gun safety, enroll in an NRA hunter clinic or state hunter education class, or an NRA safety training or basic marksmanship course.

TODAY'S AMERICAN HUNTER

If you're a hunter, you're one of 20 million Americans who love the outdoors, have a close tie with traditions, and help conserve our natural resources. You know the thrill and beauty of a duck blind at dawn, a whitetail buck sneaking past your stand, a hot-headed, bugling bull elk. With your friends and forefathers you share the rich traditions of knowing wild places and good hunting dogs. Your woodsmanship and appreciation of nature provide food for body and soul.

And through contributions to hunting licenses and stamps, conservation tax funds, and sportsman clubs, you are partly responsible for the dramatic recovery of wildlife and its habitat. Hunters can take great pride — and satisfaction that only hunters know — in the great increases of deer, turkeys, elk, some waterfowl, and other species over the last century.

Your involvement with the National Rifle Association of America is also important to promote conservation and sportsmanship. In NRA, concerned hunters and shooters work together for laws and programs of benefit to the shooting sports. Most important is the education of sportsmen through programs like the nationwide Hunter Clinic Program operated by the NRA Hunter Services Division. Through the program and the Hunter Skills Series of how-to hunting books, America's already admirable hunters can keep improving their skills, safety, responsibility, and sportsmanship to help ensure our country's rich hunting traditions flourish forever.

CONTENTS

Photo by Michael Hanback

WELCOME TO UPLAND BIRD HUNTING

Upland bird hunting is wonderful images. Bobwhite quail whirring from frosty honeysuckle, gaudy ring-necked pheasants springing noisily into brilliant autumn skies, mourning doves twisting and turning over freshly cut grainfields. A high-tailed English setter locking onto the scent of woodcock on a crisp New England morning. A springer spaniel scouring oak foothills and desert washes for elusive Western quail.

Upland bird hunting is quality sport. Bird hunters cherish fine shotguns and pridefully hone their wingshooting skills. They train well-bred, stylish gundogs to hunt effectively and conserve game. Bird hunters choose their hunting companions carefully. They spend endless off-season hours pouring over maps and walking fields and woodlands, locating prime covers and checking on brood success. During bird seasons, hunters treat their game with utmost respect.

Upland bird hunting is a splendid social event. Perhaps a family weekend for husband and wife and son or daughter to experience the myriad pleasures of the outdoors. Or an opportunity for old friends to share a day afield and an evening reminiscing of past seasons' shotguns, dogs, birds taken and shots missed. The gathering places for this fine sport are diverse — maybe a Southern dove field, a Western quail cover, a Northern grouse covert or a quality hunting preserve.

Most every hunter in North America has pursued upland gamebirds at one time or another. Each year nearly 10 million wingshooters spend over 100 million days hunting doves, quail, pheasants, grouse, prairie chickens and other upland birds. These sportsmen shell out approximately $2 billion annually in license fees, gamebird organization dues, land-lease and trespass fees, hunting dog upkeep, and travel-related expenses. Combined, this represents an invaluable financial benefit to upland gamebird management and local economies.

Upland Bird Hunting is geared to all bird hunters, novices and veterans alike, in North America. In this book you'll find practical, in-depth advice on planning hunts, gearing up, selecting gundogs, choosing shotguns and loads, and honing your wingshooting skills. There is extensive biological information on 19 species of upland birds, followed by modern strategies for hunting them successfully. You'll find pointers on handling and field dressing gamebirds, along with "four star" recipes for preparing your upland bounty. Most importantly, you'll learn how to pursue our delicately beautiful uplanders in the safest, most ethical way.

So sit back and relax. Enjoy the wonderful images of this quality sport, and use the practical information presented here to become a more skilled, well-rounded upland bird hunter.

Photo by Charles J. Farmer

Part I
Before the Hunt

Photo by Karen Lollo

CHAPTER 1

PLANNING AN UPLAND BIRD HUNT

U pland bird hunting in the United States and Canada today is a wonderfully diverse sport. Depending upon where you live, for example, you might drive an hour or so to hunt doves or woodcock for an afternoon. Then travel 100 miles one weekend to chase pheasants and quail. You might ultimately decide to drive or fly cross-country for a week-long adventure with Hungarian partridge and sharp-tailed grouse.

Regardless of logistics, whether you intend to hunt an afternoon or a week, one constant remains: To experience safe, enjoyable, successful wingshooting afield you must plan strategically before ever leaving home. Which birds will you hunt? Where will you hunt them? What licenses, maps and other materials must you obtain? Should you go alone or consider the services of an outfitter or hunting preserve? This chapter, covering these topics and more, will get you off to a flying start.

Which Birds to Hunt?

Deeper into this book you'll find specific information on no less than 19 species of upland gamebirds scattered from coast to coast, north to south, across North America. In various corners of the country, some bird seasons will be open from September through March. With such variety and seemingly unlimited opportunity, the first step in planning an effective hunting strategy lies in choosing a specific upland bird species or two to hunt.

For most hunters, availability of birds will be the deciding factor. In most cases, you will simply hunt whichever species are found in solid numbers within reasonable driving distance of your home. This is typically doves in September and pheasants or one of the species of grouse, partridge or quail later in the season. Once you have perfected your technique on local birds, you may

Photo by F.R. Martin

Photo Courtesy Florida Game and Fresh Water Fish Commission

Photo by Bob Lollo

Photo by Bob Miller, Arizona Game and Fish Department

Which birds to hunt? Begin with species abundant in your area — perhaps ruffed grouse in the North, bobwhites down South, pheasants in the Midwest, desert quail in the Southwest. Once you've perfected your technique on local birds, planning an out-of-state hunt for different species is an exciting way to broaden your horizons.

then decide to travel out of state to hunt familiar birds in fresh covers or exotic uplanders in entirely different habitat.

Choosing a bird whose beauty and habits strike your fancy will add immense pleasure to the hunt. The delicate russet beauty of the bobwhite may catch the eye of one hunter, while the gaudiness of a cock pheasant excites another. Some hunters will enjoy the twisting, erratic flight of doves, while others will prefer the straightaway thundering of a tree-dodging ruffed grouse.

Finally, your age and health must play a role if you expect to hunt safely and enjoyably afield. You must choose birds within your reach. A strong 20-year-old can hunt any species, easily scaling rugged chukar ridges or mountain grouse covers. An elderly hunter or one with a bum knee, however, may find his joy walking leisurely in prairies for sage grouse.

A Place to Hunt

Having decided which birds to hunt, the next logical step is to discover a prime place to pursue them. This can be difficult today. Modern land-development practices and clean-farming methods have changed, and reduced, upland bird habitat in many areas. In addition, access to hundreds of acres of private lands is being restricted each day. Still, the bird shooter who plans carefully, using the following tips as a guide, should be able to find a quality hunting ground.

Public Land Opportunities

Bird hunters can roam freely on millions of acres of common soil across the United States. Both federal and state public hunting areas offer myriad wingshooting opportunities.

In fact much of the finest bird hunting in the West is found on millions of acres administered by the Bureau of Land Management (BLM). BLM lands, many of them in lower elevations, provide prime habitat for doves, sage and sharp-tailed grouse, pheasants, Hungarian partridge and several species of quail.

The U. S. Forest Service administers millions of acres of National Forest scattered across the United States. Most national forests, originally established by Congress for timber production, are located in mountainous country and provide habitat for several species of uplanders, including band-tailed pigeons, chukars, woodcock and ruffed and blue grouse.

Though many hunters never realize it, public hunting is available on some National Wildlife Refuges across the country. These areas, managed by the U. S. Fish and Wildlife Service, are typically wetlands, but their woodland fringes and fields can offer excellent upland bird habitat on some of the refuge system.

After determining which federal lands are available in the area you intend to hunt, you should request specific information from a regional, district or local office of the BLM, Forest Service or Fish and Wildlife Service. Telephone numbers of local offices can be found under "U. S. Government" in your phone directory, or you can write the following headquarters for the addresses

5

and phone numbers of district offices in your area: Bureau of Land Management, 1620 L Street, NW, Washington, D.C. 20006; U. S. Forest Service, P.O. Box 2417, Washington, D.C. 20013; U. S. Fish and Wildlife Service, 1849 C Street, M5 670 ARLSQ, Washington, D.C. 20240.

Hunting can also be found on state wildlife management areas. Though state lands are smaller and more scattered than sprawling federal prairies, grasslands and forests, they can offer fair to excellent gunning for a variety of upland birds.

For information on public hunting areas in your state, contact your fish and wildlife agency. You should also consider subscribing to your state's wildlife magazine each month. You will find many articles, particularly in fall hunting issues, on top public lands within the state.

In addition to free access, state-owned public lands, many funded by sportsmen's license fees and related excise taxes, offer the upland hunter an added incentive. Both federal and state agencies, in cooperation with conservation organizations such as Quail Unlimited, Pheasants Forever and The Ruffed Grouse Society, often plant cover and food plots or help renew aging forest cover on public areas. At times, this helps to stabilize gamebird populations and provides prime cover to hunt.

Photo by Michael Hanback

State public hunting areas are typically smaller in size than federal lands, but many offer bigtime bird hunting opportunities.

So consider both federal and state lands when planning an upland bird hunt. While these areas typically host many hunters during deer and big game seasons, rarely will you find huge crowds during bird season, particularly after opening weekend. The bird hunter willing to walk can find plenty of elbow room — and often excellent wingshooting.

Private Land Privileges

While public land hunting can be excellent, there is no question that much of today's prime wingshooting is found on private farms, ranches and woodlands. The upland hunter has several options for unlocking these privileges.

Most common is simply approaching a landowner and asking courteously for permission to hunt his property. Specific tips on requesting permission and then keeping it are found in Chapter 15.

While many landowners may be reluctant to grant permission to hunt deer and big game, some will allow you to bird hunt. It never hurts to ask politely.

Consider corporate lands in your area, especially those owned by coal and timber companies. These companies typically own large tracts of land and issue daily or seasonal hunting permits for a reasonable fee. And such business operations as strip mining and clearcutting can create excellent edge habitat for bobwhite quail, ruffed and blue grouse, woodcock and other upland gamebirds.

Private hunting leases and clubs are becoming increasingly

Photo by James M. Norine

Private farms and ranches can offer excellent bird hunting. Ask politely and you may gain permission to hunt.

popular today, particularly in areas where accessible lands are dwindling. Under these agreements an individual or group of bird hunters leases hunting rights from a private landowner. Lease rates vary widely, depending on such factors as location, acreage, bird populations and number of hunters with access.

If you're interested in leasing property to hunt or joining a hunting club, check the classified ads of your local newspaper; lease opportunities often appear under "Real Estate for Rent." It is up to you, of course, whether spending hundreds of dollars to lease hunting rights is worth it. But be advised that excellent wingshooting is available on private leases today.

Do-It-Yourself Bird Hunting

After you focus upon a general hunting area in your state or province, the following tips will help you zero in on the best wingshooting opportunities.

First, secure the appropriate maps. If hunting public land, request sportsmen's maps from the appropriate federal, state or provincial agency. If hunting private property, visit the local government center and scan local maps and plat books; these show roads, property boundaries and prominent landmarks. Then invest in topographical maps of the hunting area. Not only will a variety of maps allow you to find your way and hunt safely and legally within the proper boundaries, they can also unlock prime bird hunting covers. Learn to map read strategically and you may discover a secluded, seldom-hunted creek bottom, clearcut, drainage ditch or hollow teeming with birds.

You should obtain as much information as possible from your state or provincial wildlife agency. Request a copy of the hunting regulations (you should receive these upon purchasing your bird license) and any other brochures published specifically for sportsmen. As mentioned, subscribe to your state's wildlife magazine. Combined, all of this information will prove invaluable when planning both in-state and out-of-state bird hunts.

All states and provinces have resident gamebird biologists. Phone your agency and ask to speak with him or her. This is a vital part of the planning process, as upland gamebird populations can vary widely from year to year, from cover to cover, depending on such natural factors as drought, excessive rainfall, hard winters and predation. An agency's fall forecast can give you the latest scoop on bird population numbers and predicted harvests in the area you plan to hunt.

Photo Courtesy Wildlife Management Institute

When exploring places to hunt, consider recent land-use practices. While development and clean-farming have reduced bobwhite, pheasant and prairie chicken habitat in many areas, strip mining and clearcutting have created excellent edge cover for grouse and other woodland birds.

Chat with local conservation officers and gun shop personnel. They may offer advice on where to focus your hunting. Finally, speak with an experienced bird hunter in the area if possible. Rarely will he reveal his favorite coverts, and you shouldn't expect him to! But perhaps he might provide firsthand knowledge of the type of cover you should hunt and the techniques you should employ afield.

It is common for an individual or group to travel to a neighboring state, or even cross-country, for a taste of "fresh" bird hunting in new covers. While the previous information certainly applies, consider these additional trip-planning tips.

Plan early. Well in advance of your hunt obtain all necessary regulations, maps and brochures from the fish and game agency of the state or Canadian province you will visit. Call ahead and speak with a biologist for bird counts and hunting forecasts.

Government-run tourism departments and chambers of commerce are excellent sources of information. They can provide lists of motels, campgrounds, airports and rental car firms that may fit into your travel plans.

In most states and provinces, non-resident upland bird hunting licenses are unlimited and available over the counter from

Photo by Michael Hanback

When planning a hunt in unfamiliar country, chat with a local wing-shooter if possible. Rarely will he reveal his favorite covers, but he might point you in the general direction of birds.

licensing agents. Remember that some states and provinces require hunter education certification for all hunters or youngsters. Some require proof of having held a valid hunting license in the past. Be sure to check the regulations beforehand and carry the necessary documents when you go.

Finally, obtain information on normal weather conditions during the time period you wish to hunt. Having knowledge of weather forecasts immediately prior to departure is invaluable for proper planning.

Outfitted Bird Hunts

For the traveling bird hunter, hiring an outfitter is often advantageous. A quality guide knows the country and often has access to prime private-land covers. He is familiar with the habits of the local gamebirds and has perfected his technique for hunting them. He has well-trained dogs for the job. He offers lodging, meals and transportation. In short, he does the work while you concentrate on the hunting and shooting.

Many lodges and camps across North America specialize in *wild* bird hunting today. Ruffed grouse and woodcock outfits are found in the North Country. Midwestern guides specialize in native pheasant hunting. Western outfitters offer opportunities for sharp-tailed and sage grouse, pheasants, chukars and

Hungarian partridge. Lodges in the South and Southwest cater to quail hunters. Phenomenal dove shooting can be found at Southern plantations and resorts south of the border.

Only you can decide if spending $250 or more to hire a guide is worth the bird hunting you will glean in return. If this is your choice, consider these tips on locating an honest, reputable outfitter.

A state or provincial wildlife agency or local chamber of commerce can provide a listing of resident guides. You can also check the classified ads in the back pages of your favorite outdoor magazines for lodges, outfitters and hunting preserves.

One of the best ways to hire any guide or outfitter is through a hunting consultant or booking agent who represents a number of outfitters. You tell the agent which species of birds interest you, where you wish to hunt and what you expect from the experience. The consultant then tailors a personalized hunt for you. And since the outfitter pays the consultant's fees, your cost is the same whether you book through an outfitter or agent.

Most hunting consultants and outfitters are reputable and honest today. Some, sadly, are not. Thoroughly check the credentials of any agent, outfitter or guide before shelling out a penny.

Call state or provincial wildlife agencies, and ask if an outfitter has been charged with any game-law violations. If so, don't patronize them. Call or write the consultant or guide, and request references. Call these hunters, asking every imaginable question. Inquire about the consultant's or outfitter's attitude and knowledge. Ask about the accommodations, hunting area,

Photo by Michael Hanback

Many outfitters across North America cater to traveling bird hunters. In the South you might book a plantation-style quail hunt, complete with mule-drawn wagons, stylish pointers and fast-rising native bobwhites.

abundance of birds, techniques employed and quality of dogs. Finally, well before the hunt get in writing all fees and services to be provided by the agent or outfitter. Do your homework and chances are you won't be disappointed, but will be treated to the upland bird hunt of a lifetime.

Hunting Preserves

Most of the writing up to this point has focused on hunting native birds on open lands. But any discussion of places to hunt must include licensed hunting preserves — commercial operations that release pen-raised pheasants, quail or partridges and charge hunters to shoot them.

Preserves have been around for hundreds of years. They are now growing in leaps and bounds, enjoying a popularity boom in many areas.

In the early years, some of these operations were "shooting preserves" that deserved the tainted reputation they got. These early preserves charged shooters only for the number of dead birds bagged. Undeniably, the economics of such an operation forced some early operators to provide a hunt that was less than a challenge. But today, private-enterprise hunting preserves have done well because they've cleaned up their act by improving their game management techniques.

These businesses offer opportunities for people from the cities or suburbs who have few places to hunt. They promise action

Photo by John Mullin, North American Gamebird Association

Hunting preserves located near cities and suburbs are becoming increasingly popular. These operations offer guides, dogs and wingshooting for quail, pheasants and chukars.

and can be excellent training grounds for young shotgunners. They offer leisurely hunting for the elderly or handicapped. Because they typically provide lunch, and perhaps lodging, guides and well-trained dogs, they can be a convenient option for any hunter simply wishing a no-hassle day afield. Some preserves even have training fields where you can pay to plant a few birds and train your own dog.

Modern hunting preserves vary widely, from a couple hundred acres near major Eastern cities to 30,000 acres in Texas. Some are private and *very* expensive. Others, open to the public, offer a half or full day's shooting for $50 and up.

Hunting preserves provide hunting over special extended seasons, which in some states run year-round. In a few states, no state hunting license is required on these managed areas. Daily bag limits are selected by the individual hunter. Therefore, preserves must propagate and restock gamebirds.

The gamebirds are for the most part pen-raised, but most hunting preserves provide fine nesting cover and escape cover for native gamebird species. Preserves encourage natural reproduction in these game coverts, but can't rely on mother nature to provide all the birds.

Quality hunting preserves restock flighty gamebirds in tailor-made wildlife habitat that's planned and planted for hunting. The hunting is challenging because there is often more wildlife habitat and escape cover on a good hunting preserve than there is on an average farm—after crops have been harvested.

Some preserves stock gamebirds that might not normally be available to hunters in a particular region. But remember, many species hunted during regular hunting seasons were never native to the United States and Canada. Ring-necked pheasants, chukar partridge and Hungarian partridge have all been introduced into North America.

Most modern hunting preserves now charge for the total experience instead of basing fees solely on dead birds bagged. Most hunting preserves now offer package plans, charging by the hunt.

Most preserves no longer guarantee that you'll bag a specified number of birds. They charge by the hunt—either for a half-day experience, or a full-day package opportunity.

There is no doubt that the price of supporting improved habitat and quality hunting is a little chilling to the hunter who has never kept a list of expenses, such as travel, lodging, licenses, and hunting dog upkeep, during "free" hunting experiences. But sportsmen who keep tabs on all their hunting expenses may find preserve charges well within reason.

Directories of hunting preserves are available from state or provincial wildlife agencies. A national directory of hunting preserves is available by writing the National Shooting Sports Foundation, 555 Danbury Road, Wilton, CT 06897, or by calling (203) 762-1320.

When inquiring about hunting preserves, be sure to request brochures and references. Contact references and ask about the attitudes of the operators and their staff. Get opinions on the total hunting experience, including habitat, quality of the dogs and handlers and bird flight.

You may have to shop around for a preserve that fits your tastes, desires and pocketbook, but don't knock the concept until you have tried a few. The ultimate goal of any preserve is to simulate bird hunting as it would occur in the wild. The quality of the quail or pheasants — their strength and stamina in flight — is what makes or breaks a day of preserve shooting.

Photo by Joe Workosky

Whether on public or private lands, pursuing upland birds is a great way to bring families into hunting and outdoor recreation.

Personal Fitness

Upland bird hunting varies widely, from a slow, leisurely stroll for woodcock or grouse, to a fast, strenuous track meet for desert quail or chukars. Regardless, one fact remains: Bird hunters walk a lot, sometimes five, eight, 10 miles a day. Getting into good physical condition will help ensure safe, pleasant days afield.

Good exercises for the upland hunter include walking, jogging and hiking. Cardiovascular exercises such as cycling and swimming are excellent routines for the hunter. Most fitness experts suggest 20 to 30 minutes of aerobic exercise at least three times a week. Working out with light weights will tone your upper body as well, increasing your strength and stamina.

Before embarking on any exercise routine, medical experts suggest that everyone undergo a complete physical. This is especially important if you are over age 30, have a history of health problems or take medication regularly.

Photo by Mike Strandlund

Working out in summer allows you to hunt safely and enjoyably come fall. Walking, jogging, cycling and swimming are excellent aerobic exercises for the hard-walking bird hunter.

Once in reasonably good shape, bird hunt a lot. By season's end you'll be lean and tough from all the walking. It's of utmost importance to continue exercising in the off season to maintain this level of fitness acquired from miles of hiking the uplands.

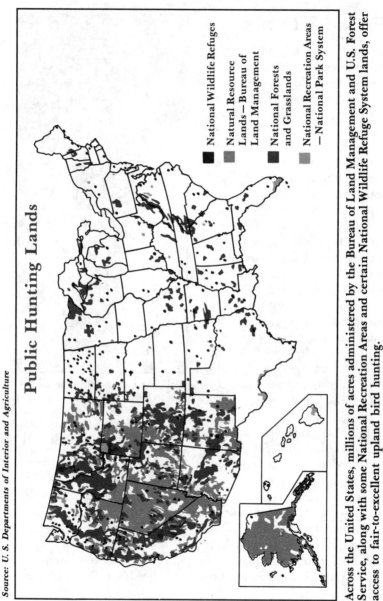

Public Hunting Lands

Legend:
- National Wildlife Refuges
- Natural Resource Lands — Bureau of Land Management
- National Forests and Grasslands
- National Recreation Areas — National Park System

Source: U. S. Departments of Interior and Agriculture

Across the United States, millions of acres administered by the Bureau of Land Management and U.S. Forest Service, along with some National Recreation Areas and certain National Wildlife Refuge System lands, offer access to fair-to-excellent upland bird hunting.

CHAPTER 2

GEARING UP FOR UPLAND BIRDS

Photo by Hank Andrews

The well-dressed bird hunter can walk safely and comfortably for miles.

Compared to other types of hunting, the pursuit of upland birds is not a gear-oriented sport. Regardless of where and which species of gamebirds you hunt, never will you need equipment as extensive as that of the waterfowl, wild turkey or big game hunter. Still, wearing the proper clothing and carrying a reasonable amount of essentials will ensure an enjoyable, safe and successful outing.

Clothing

Upland birds are hunted in a variety of habitats and weather conditions across North America. For example, early season in the desert, western quail hunters may perspire profusely beneath a sizzling sun. In Appalachian ruffed grouse covers in late January, hunters may shiver amid snow and sub-freezing temperatures. On Canadian sharp-tailed prairies, the fickle October weather may be clear and warm one day, snowy and frigid the next.

The point is no single clothing system is tailor-made for the great diversity of bird hunting conditions you might encounter. The key to hunting comfortably, safely and effectively is to plan

Photos by Michael Hanback

Upland birds are hunted in a variety of conditions, so a hunter must tailor his or her clothing to the weather. Jeans and a T-shirt might suffice for September doves, while warm layers are essential on a late-season grouse hunt.

your outings carefully, matching your clothes to your specific pursuit of birds.

Underwear and Outerwear

For hunting doves, band-tailed pigeons, chukars and some species of western grouse in September and October, jeans or khaki pants may suffice. For most warm-weather situations, however, such as when walking bobwhite, pheasant, woodcock or grouse cover in early fall, lightweight brush pants are best.

When it's hot, a bird hunter can often get by with a T-shirt. A long-sleeved, lightweight cotton shirt is a more practical choice, however. You can roll up the sleeves when you start to sweat, or roll them down to protect your arms from briars, heavy brush or biting flies.

Photo by Ron Spomer

Late in the season, lightweight longjohns are excellent for the hard-walking bird hunter. Pull wool sweater and pants over this "sweat-wicking" underwear, and you'll stay comfortable and warm.

October through January, when the air turns crisp to cold and frost or snow shimmers in the bird covers, is the most popular and invigorating time of year to hunt upland birds across North America. From a clothing standpoint, it is the time to begin layering your underwear and outerwear for comfortable walking and shooting.

Lightweight longjohns, preferably woven of silk or one of today's high-tech fabrics like polypropylene or Thermax, which "wick" perspiration away from your body, thus keeping you dry, warm and comfortable, are best for the upland bird hunter. When trekking miles for birds, heavyweight cotton, down or Thinsulate longjohns will make you sweat profusely, even in frigid temperatures.

You have a number of options for layering over this underwear. In cool climates, medium-weight brush pants and a lightweight chamois or woolen shirt should keep you comfortable.

On bitter-cold days afield, you should opt for heavyweight brush pants or lightweight wool pants under chaps. Two chamois or woolen shirts, perhaps topped with a sweater or lightweight fleece jacket, can be worn on sub-freezing mornings. For the bird shooter, this layering system is more efficient than wearing a heavy down- or synthetic-insulated coat or parka. Not only will layered upper-body clothing keep you adequately warm, it is streamlined enough to promote the smooth shouldering and swinging of your shotgun on fast-rising birds. A parka may keep you warm but catch the buttstock of your shotgun and inhibit your swing.

Layering your outerwear has an added advantage. You can regulate your body temperature and comfort level while walking. If midday temperatures rise and you begin to sweat, shirts can be peeled off and stored in your gunning coat or game vest. If afternoon temperatures plummet, you can pull out an extra shirt to break the chill.

Brush Pants and Chaps

To protect your shins and thighs from slashing briars, brambles and blowdowns, you need at least one good pair of brush pants or chaps.

Brush pants come in a variety of styles and colors. The most popular ones are constructed of tough, durable cotton duck and are available in light, medium and heavy weights, either lined or unlined. Others are simply lightweight cotton, poplin or twill trousers faced with briar-proof nylon, canvas or pigskin. Brown,

Photo by Michael Hanback

While one bird hunter might prefer brush pants (left), another may opt for the look and feel of chaps (right). Either will protect your shins and thighs from briars and brambles.

tan and olive are choice colors; some are patterned in various camouflage.

If you typically bird hunt early in the season, in a warm-weather clime, or on grasslands and open prairies choose lightweight brush pants. The thinnest canvas pants or poplin trousers faced with nylon will protect you adequately in brush, yet "breathe," allowing you to hunt coolly and comfortably.

If you plan to bust thick, heavy, thorny brush and typically hunt late into bird season, select medium- or heavyweight pants. Thick duck pants with reinforced legs, while often heavy, offer maximum protection from briars and the elements. Flannel- or chamois-lined brush pants are warm and excellent for winter bird hunting.

A final point: When wearing heavyweight brush pants consider strapping on suspenders. These will keep the pants riding high and snugly, allowing you to walk comfortably.

Nylon chaps are popular with many bird hunters because of their convenience; with zippered bottoms, they are easily slipped over jeans, khakis or wool pants. Chaps are cool, lightweight and comfortable, yet durable enough to turn heavy brush and sharp thorns. Snake-proof models, designed to thwart fangs, are available and may prove a comfortable alternative to heavy snake boots for southern and southwestern bird hunters.

Coats and Vests

For some, the classic European tweed comes to mind when talking about a bird hunting coat. For others, the brown canvas coat is the choice. While the gunning vest predominates in the uplands today, the coat still has its place.

Photo by Michael Hanback

The brown canvas coat, for years a classic in North American uplands, is still practical for bird hunters today. A quality coat is durable and provides the ultimate upper-body protection, turning briars, light rain and snow.

The pros of the bird hunting coat? It has large, deep shell pockets and a sizable, easy-access rear game bag. It provides maximum upper-body and arm protection in the thickest brush. It adequately breaks cold wind and turns away light rain and snow.

The cons? A coat is often stiff, heavy and hot. Many hunters feel a coat restricts upper-body movement and inhibits swinging a shotgun smoothly.

On the market today are a number of quality jackets and coats designed for bird hunting. While many are woven of traditional cotton duck, others are crafted from modern, lightweight yet durable materials, like nylon and Supplex. The best ones are stylish and cut full in the shoulders.

Try on a coat or jacket, preferably a size larger than you normally wear. Then bend as if you were bucking brush and swing an imaginary shotgun. If the coat feels comfortable, consider it, for it will serve you well in a variety of bird hunting situations.

Two styles of gunning vests are popular today. First is the traditional over-the-shoulder vest. Second is the game bag, which features two-inch shoulder straps and shell pockets and rear bird bag that ride low around the waist.

Crafted of the same tough, durable materials used in hunting coats, both types of vests are practical afield, providing upper-body protection in brush, yet allowing you to move your arms freely. Try on several brands and select a vest that is, of foremost importance, comfortable. Then look for large pockets with flaps; you won't lose shells when climbing fences or ducking under brush.

Both coats and vests are available in several colors today: tan, olive, brown, camouflage and hunter orange. Choice of color is up to you, but consider an orange vest if you typically hunt in extremely thick brush or dog-hair timber; this promotes safe hunting, particularly on crowded public lands. Also, many states and provinces have hunter-orange requirements for bird hunters, necessitating the choice of a hunter orange coat or vest.

Two other bird carriers are worth mentioning. One is simply a belt with attached nylon pockets and game bag that snug the hips. The other is a leather strap with loops for carrying birds; this is either slung across your shoulder or attached to your belt. While these bird carriers offer no brush protection, they are lightweight and promote free, easy walking. They can be good choices for the dove hunter, the western grouse hunter who treks

Photo by Joe Workosky

When choosing a gunning vest, make certain it fits properly — loose but snug enough to promote smooth shotgun swing. A vest should feature roomy side pockets for shells and accessories and a large, easily accessible game bag for carrying birds, lunch and spare jacket.

miles of rolling prairies and grasslands, and the chukar or band-tailed pigeon hunter who climbs steep, open mountains.

Hats

A baseball-style cap is perfect for most upland bird hunting situations. Early in the season, or when hunting anytime in warm weather, consider a cap with a long, firm brim and mesh backing; the brim shades your eyes from the sun's glare, and heat escapes through the mesh, keeping you cool. Insulated and fleece caps with ear flaps are available for cold-weather hunting.

Round, short-brimmed hats are popular with many bird hunters. They are stylish in the uplands and provide maximum visibility, though they offer little eye shading in harsh sunlight. Felt crushers give decent eyeshade, and are soft enough to give and not be ripped off in thick brush.

Hats are available in a myriad of colors, but all bird hunters should consider wearing hunter orange. The high visibility of

Photo by Michael Hanback

A cap with a sun-shielding brim is excellent. Wear safety-orange on most bird hunts, camouflage when gunning doves. Leather shooting gloves not only protect your hands from cold weather and briars, but ensure a firm grip on your shotgun. Every upland hunter must wear quality shooting glasses. They'll protect your precious eyes from slashing limbs and briars, and turn errant pellets fired from across a dove field.

an orange cap is a wonderful safety precaution anytime, and a necessity when hunting in close, thick cover. Such a hat often satisfies a wildlife agency's safety requirements.

Gloves

Even when bird hunting in warm to hot weather, consider wearing a pair of lightweight deerskin or leather shooting gloves. They will protect your hands from slashing briars, and ensure a secure grip on your shotgun.

Gloves are a necessity in cold weather. Again, deerskin or leather models, with inner insulation, are best. These gloves will keep your fingers adequately warm. They are supple and thin enough to allow you to find a shotgun's trigger with ease.

Cotton and wool gloves will suffice in a pinch for cold-weather bird hunting, though a shotgun's fore-end will often slip around on their slick surfaces, possibly creating a safety hazard. Some modern styles feature non-slip palm grips to alleviate this problem.

In cold climates some wingshooters wear fingerless wool gloves, especially on their shooting hands. Others simply wear one leather, cotton or wool glove on their off hand and leave their shooting hand ungloved. If you feel uncomfortable shooting in gloves, experiment with these options.

Footwear

Bird hunters walk a lot — it is simply the nature of the sport. So the socks and boots you wear can make or break your hunt.

While often overlooked, wearing the proper socks is the first step in keeping your feet dry, warm and blister free. White cotton socks topped with wool-nylon models in cool to cold weather are popular and have served hunters well for years. But better for the hard-walking bird hunter is a sock-layering system incorporating today's high-tech fabrics.

The system begins with a pair of underliners, thin, 10-inch, polypropylene stockings. By design these liners wick perspiration to an outer sock, thus keeping your feet dry and warm. They hug each foot snugly, reducing chafing, rubbing and blistering.

In warm to cool weather these underliners are topped with lightweight wool, Thermax or polypropylene socks. Heavyweight wool or polypropylene socks are available for the coldest bird hunting conditions.

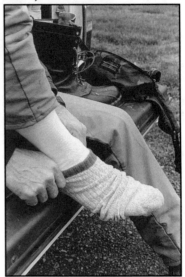

Photo by Michael Hanback

Layering socks, by pulling wool over thin, sweat-wicking underliners, keeps feet dry, warm and blister-free.

These high-tech socks unquestionably cost more than standard cottons and wool-nylon blends. A single sock "system" can run $10 or more, but may well be worth it. At the end of a long, hard day walking cornfields, prairies, woodlands or mountains, your feet will still be dry and comfortable.

The upland bird hunter has a choice of three basic boot designs: leather, rubber or a combination of the two.

Thin, uninsulated leather boots with supple eight-inch uppers and thin crepe soles are excellent for early-season hunting. They are lightweight, cool and comfortable, perfect for leisurely walking in flat or rolling bird country. These boots are a fine choice for dove hunters, and for years have been popular on Southern bobwhite plantations and in Northern grouse coverts.

Thick leather boots with sturdy lug or Air-Bob soles are best for hunting rugged bird terrain. They offer protection from prickly cacti and rocks in the desert, and provide good traction when climbing in mountains. Many excellent models from a

Photo by Mike Strandlund

When hunting rugged bird country, select stout leather boots with quality soles. These protect your feet and ankles from desert cacti and rocks, and provide good traction when climbing mountains.

NRA Staff Photo

Rubber-bottomed boots with leather or nylon uppers are popular with upland hunters. Uppers provide adequate ankle support, while bottoms turn water, mud and snow.

variety of manufacturers are available with waterproof Gore-Tex liners, Thinsulate insulation and Cordura nylon uppers. These are popular, versatile boots, easily tailored to a variety of bird hunting habitats and weather conditions.

A note on purchasing and wearing leather boots. Select a style that pleases your eye and best suits your type of bird hunting. Then spend as much as you can afford on the boots, from $50 to $200. Break them in well before the season. Treat them with silicone, oil or paste. Chances are they will keep your feet dry, comfortable and healthy for years in the uplands.

While popular and stylish in Europe, calf- or knee-high rubber boots have limited use in North American uplands. They fit loosely (though the best ones are "ankle-fit") and can cause your feet to sweat heavily when walking even moderate distances. Still, a minority of southern bobwhite hunters swear by them. And they are the ultimate water boots. Woodcock and snipe hunters may find them just the ticket for sloshing short distances through marshes and bogs.

Rubber-bottomed or gum boots with leather or Cordura nylon uppers are in style with bird hunters today. The uppers provide ankle support and allow the boots to breathe, while the rubber bottoms turn water, mud and snow.

With standard chain-link soles, these boots provide adequate traction for pheasant, quail, woodcock and most types of grouse hunting. Some manufacturers have put lug and Air-Bob soles on these boots to offer maximum footing, which are best for the mountain bird hunter.

One drawback has always been that rubber-bottomed boots chill your toes in cold weather. Manufacturers have added removable, insulated liners to many models, making them versatile and a fine choice for most types of bird hunting early autumn through winter.

Finally, bird hunters in the desert Southwest, western prairies and Deep South might need snake boots. While these leather, calf-high boots are typically hot and cumbersome, they provide peace of mind when hunting in warm-weather habitats where rattlesnakes or cottonmouths may be encountered. With your feet, ankles and calves encased securely in these boots, you can concentrate on quail hunting rather than searching for snakes in the grass.

Foul-Weather Gear

From early autumn through winter, rain and snow are common in the uplands of North America. While few upland birds are hunted seriously in driving rains, chances are every hunter will get caught out in a storm or squall sometime during the season. To hunt effectively then is to stay dry and warm, so you should have on hand or in your vehicle adequate rain gear.

Consider both rain jacket and pants. A jacket is obvious because it keeps your torso dry and warm. While many hunters forego the pants, they will keep your legs, especially your thighs, dry when walking through soggy, dripping fields and woodlands.

You have three basic choices. Many hunters can get by with standard plastic or coated-nylon rain wear. These are relatively

Photo by Michael Hanback

Chances are you'll get caught out in rain or wet snow sometime during bird season. Quality rain jacket and pants will help you weather the storm.

inexpensive suits, about $30 to $60, and turn water effectively on short, easy hunts. These can, however, cause you to sweat when walking in warm weather. Plastic and nylon may also rip and shred in heavy brush and thorns.

Gore-Tex is a popular waterproof fabric woven into a variety of tough, durable, modern materials. It "breathes," allowing perspiration to escape; this helps keep you dry and warm. Gore-Tex rain wear is expensive, with a suit easily costing over $200, but is an excellent choice for any wingshooter who hunts extensively in nasty weather.

Finally, oiled/waxed cotton rain wear is becoming increasingly popular with upland bird hunters today. Not only is this dark-green or brown outerwear stylish, it is waterproof, tough, breathable and fully cut, which allows you to hunt freely and swing a shotgun smoothly. Coats with rear game bags and deep shell pockets, jackets, pants and hats are available. Though expensive — you could pay as much $300 to $400 for a suit — these waxed-cotton garments are fine choices for the serious upland hunter.

Bird Hunting Accessories

Shooting Glasses

Every upland bird hunter must wear quality shooting glasses. These will protect your precious eyes in the unlikely, but always possible, event of a shotshell rupturing upon firing. Good glasses will deflect errant pellets fired across a dove field. They will also protect your eyes from all sorts of annoying and dangerous hazards in bird country. Quality lenses repel dirt, dust, grit and rain. If tinted, shooting glasses block a major portion of the sun's damaging ultraviolet rays. Lenses turn face-lashing thorns and tree limbs.

Quality shooting glasses have an added advantage. Available in a number of tints, they provide definition and contrast in a variety of light conditions. Matching tints to changing light allows you to focus sharply on flying birds, thus improving your shooting. Most popular among bird hunters are gray and green lenses; they are perfect for clear, sunny days, or when sunlight shimmers brightly on snow. Yellow and vermillion tints are ideal for rainy or overcast days, or when hunting in dense, low-light forests.

Some manufacturers offer frames with a variety of clear and shaded lenses that can be interchanged according to these variable conditions.

When selecting shooting glasses, first check the lenses. They should be made of high-impact glass, plastic, thermoplastic or polycarbonate, and large enough to cover your eyes completely. Brow bars and padded ear loops ensure a snug, comfortable fit.

Some manufacturers can add prescription lenses to their frames. Flip-up protective lenses can be conveniently clipped to your prescription glasses.

Field Gear

Every hunter should carry a knife. For the bird shooter, a small, lightweight, well-sharpened pocketknife is adequate. A compact, folding bird knife with a locking blade and curved gut hook for dressing birds can be handy.

Even when hunting close to home or vehicle, a wingshooter should carry essentials in his gunning coat or vest. Spare eyeglasses or contact lenses are an obvious must and can be easily slipped

Photo by Michael Hanback

On a bird hunt close to home, camp or vehicle, carry a knife, basic first-aid gear, eye-care products, water and snack. When trekking far off the beaten path, add survival necessities such as flashlight, matches, map and compass.

into a shirt pocket. Bandages for briar cuts and aspirin for headaches can ensure an enjoyable day afield.

When hunting upland birds in rattler or cottonmouth country, consider a modern snake-bite kit, but check first with a physician. Many medical experts now shun treating snake bites in the field.

When trekking far from your vehicle in big or unfamiliar country, as you will on many bird hunts out west and up north, carry a small survival or first-aid kit including matches and a small flashlight. These are safety necessities in late fall and winter, when days grow short and the weather can change in the blink of an eye. A high-quality compass and topographical maps are beneficial, and not only for finding your way. Learn to read a topographical map effectively, and you can often discover prime, secluded, seldom-hunted bird covers.

On all hunts carry in your coat or vest a bottle of water. A hard-walking bird hunter can dehydrate quickly, not only in warm weather but on cold days as well. Lunch and a snack will provide energy, keeping you moving along and hunting effectively.

Finally, don't forget your bird hunting license or stamps. Check your local regulations. A few states require bird licenses to be carried in a holder and pinned to your gunning coat or vest.

Special Considerations

While the aforementioned gear will serve you well on most upland bird hunts, some situations are unique. For example, if you will be traveling to a faraway lodge, carry several sets of hunting and camp clothes and extensive personal gear. If you plan a camping excursion for birds (common and popular out west during the splendid months of September and October) you will need a tent, sleeping bag, food, cooler, cooking utensils, tools and other gear. One beauty of upland bird hunting is that the sport offers a variety of opportunities in wonderfully diverse country. Plan your hunt carefully and tailor your gear requirements to the wingshooting at hand.

Gear for Women

The point was made earlier that no single clothing system is tailor-made for the great diversity of bird hunting conditions. This becomes more obvious if you are a woman. In many cases you will find difficulty in matching, not to mention purchasing, your clothes for upland bird hunting.

Women should look for brush pants with an elastic waistband in the back to provide a comfortable fit.

The search for a hunting coat or vest may cause somewhat more of a problem. While many sporting goods retailers stock men's small or medium sizes, these are often too tight. Therefore, women generally have to buy a larger size and then have alterations made. An inexpensive alternative to layering socks is to wear nylon pantyhose or tights under cotton or wool socks. An added pair of support hose can make walking more comfortable.

Currently, most manufacturers feel there is not a large enough market to produce women's hunting clothing, and very few sporting good stores stock them. However, they are available if you know where to look.

In an effort to assist women in search of comfortable hunting gear, the NRA Women's Issues and Information Division offers a *Women's Products Resource List.* This includes a list of manufacturers of firearms, clothing, footwear and other accessories specially designed or recommended for women's hunting and shooting needs.

Equipment Considerations

In summarizing bird hunting gear, the following "quick-see" list of clothing and accessories should ensure a comfortable, safe, successful day in the uplands:

- **Brush Pants or Chaps**
- **Gunning Coat or Game Vest**
- **Silk or Polypropylene Underwear**
- **Cotton, Flannel, or Chamois Shirt**
- **Extra Shirts, Sweater and Lightweight Fleece Jacket**
- **Underliner and Wool or Polypropylene Socks**
- **Leather or Rubber-Bottomed Boots**
- **Snake Boots (If Necessary)**
- **Hunter Orange Cap**
- **Tanned-Leather Shooting Gloves**
- **Rain Wear**
- **Shooting Glasses**
- **Pocketknife**
- **Small Survival or First-Aid Kit**
- **Spare Corrective Lenses (Glasses/Contacts)**
- **Matches**
- **Small Flashlight**
- **Compass**
- **Topographic Maps**
- **Water, Lunch and Snack**
- **Shotgun and Extra Shells**
- **Hunting License**

CHAPTER 3

GUNDOGS FOR UPLAND BIRDS

The sleek, lemon-ticked setter bitch quarters the frost-tipped corn stubble. She holds her head high as she runs, her nose catching the crisp morning air. Her tail floats like a grand feather in the wisp of autumn breeze. Suddenly she whirls and freezes on three legs. The hunter, heart pounding, slips in behind the dog, until the covey of bobwhites whirs away in a gentle roar. The report of the shotgun rocks the sleepy countryside. A quail folds neatly. Upon command, the setter breaks, then returns to drop the russet bird delicately into the hunter's waiting hand.

Photo by Leonard Lee Rue III

Not only will a well-trained gundog help you find more birds, its style, grace and beauty afield will add immense pleasure to your hunting.

For legions of bird hunters across North America, herein lies the very essence of sport. For them no more beautiful, more invigorating, more satisfying sight exists than a well-trained gundog in action on a crisp autumn morning, running with style and finding birds for the gun. In the wake of such a splendid scenario, shooting a bird becomes secondary, though the recovery of fallen game makes the hunt complete.

While many species of upland gamebirds can be hunted with varying degrees of success without a dog—by hunters who simply walk fields, prairies or woodland coverts, kicking up birds—a trained bird dog will unquestionably lead to more effective hunting. Too, a classy gundog running with a big heart and an overwhelming desire to please adds immense pleasure and excitement to a hunter's day afield. Then there is the all-important ethical consideration: A well-trained gundog conserves game. Hunt behind a finished dog with a keen nose and instincts, and

Photo by Mike Strandlund

While training your dog to hunt correctly, emphasis should be placed on retrieving downed gamebirds.

rarely will you lose a wounded bird that runs and buries beneath thick cover. Even cleanly killed birds with camouflaged colors can be difficult to find in dense vegetation or woods. A gundog will help you locate most every upland gamebird you shoot.

The Two-Fold Investment

After contemplating the benefits of hunting with a dog, you seriously consider purchasing one. First consider this: To own an upland bird dog is to take upon yourself great responsibility. It requires a two-fold, long-term investment.

As for cost, you'll pay hundreds of dollars for a puppy or started dog. Keep the canine for years, and you'll spend additional thousands on food, veterinary bills, housing, perhaps boarding when you vacation, training tools, pen-raised birds, professional trainer's fees (if applicable) and more.

Then there is the time factor. You must spend hours, days, years solidifying a bond with your dog as you train it for hunting.

Photo by Michael Hanback

If thinking of buying a bird dog, you must commit to the two-fold investment. You'll shell out lots of money for food, housing and veterinary bills. You'll spend days, weeks and years bonding with the dog as you train it for hunting.

To keep the dog happy, healthy and in shape, you must exercise it daily in the off season and hunt it regularly during bird season.

A lot to consider. If you are not prepared to undertake these monetary and personal commitments with enthusiasm and dedication, either hunt alone or with a partner who keeps a gundog. Forget about owning one yourself. It is not fair to you if you lack the commitment, for you will find a dog more of a hassle than a blessing, and it certainly is not fair to a dog bred for a long, prosperous lifetime of hunting birds.

Selecting a Breed

Having committed to owning a gundog, the next step is to choose a breed that is right for you. To enjoy a dog and hunt it effectively, you must select a breed whose hunting mode, temperament and characteristics suit your hunting and lifestyle.

Begin by asking yourself this question: "For the covers and birds I hunt, will I do best with a pointing or flushing breed?"

Pointing dogs are without question the most popular upland bird finders in North America. They're stylish and graceful, a joy to watch. Upon locating game, they instinctively point and should hold until the hunter slips in behind to flush the birds

Photo by Dave Murrian, Tennessee Wildlife Resources Agency

Pointing dogs hunt stylishly, then freeze upon finding birds. A breed like the English setter handles most upland birds well, and is especially adept at pointing and honoring bobwhites, woodcock and grouse.

Photo by Joe Workosky

Flushing dogs are trained to quarter close in front of hunters and put birds into the air within shotgun range. The most popular breed is the English springer spaniel, a favorite of pheasant hunters.

and shoot. The best pointing dogs then become better-than-adequate retrievers, locating and bringing downed birds to hand.

Pointing breeds like the pointer, English setter and Brittany have long been the choice of bobwhite quail, ruffed grouse and woodcock hunters. Today, pointing dogs from strong hunting bloodlines will perform adequately, even splendidly, on most species of upland gamebirds.

Flushing dogs are trained to quarter close in front of the hunter and, upon making and finding game, put up birds within shotgun range. They excel at trailing and flushing running birds. Best known of the flushing breeds is the English springer spaniel, a long-time favorite of pheasant hunters.

The Labrador and golden retriever, renowned waterfowl breeds, are gaining in popularity with pheasant and western grouse hunters, and have found a niche in northern and eastern ruffed grouse and woodcock coverts. The versatile retrievers can be excellent choices for the hunter who splits time between blinds and uplands; a Lab or golden can fetch doves and wood ducks in September and October, perform adequately in upland covers in November and retrieve big ducks and geese later in the season.

The cover you hunt should also be a determining factor in the breed of gundog you select. In many parts of the country, upland bird habitat is changing, even shrinking, today. If you are a typical modern foot-hunter who covers 40-acre fields or small woodlands, you will do best with a methodical, close-ranging, easy-to-handle dog.

If, on the other hand, you typically hunt broad horizons— Western prairies, large tracts of Southern broomsedge or sprawling Midwestern cornfields—a big-running dog may best suit your bird hunting. A pointer or English setter who ranges far and wide will help you cover lots of country and find more birds each day.

Consider also a breed whose temperament and characteristics fit nicely with yours. If you plan to keep the dog in your house, you would do well to choose an affectionate, sensitive breed that is gentle and loving with children. Many professional trainers agree that this builds a solid foundation between dog and hunter, leading to better communication afield.

Size can also be a factor. Small to medium-sized dogs, 35 to 50 pounds, are most easily kept and cared for in the home.

All breeds of upland bird dogs can be kennelled outdoors, preferably in a long run with an easy-to-wash-and-disinfect concrete floor and sheltered house. Some breeds, however, adapt better than others to outside housing.

Consider trainability. Some breeds of bird dogs are simply easier to break than others. If you have little spare time or live in a city or suburb where training fields are limited, you should opt for a manageable breed, one that responds easily to training. If time and facilities are unlimited, you might find great fun, challenge and satisfaction in training and finishing the most difficult gundog.

With these thoughts in mind, let's examine the most popular upland bird dogs.

Pointing Breeds

Pointer

Muscular, deep-chested and broad-headed, yet with a streamlined overall physique, the pointer is a picture-perfect blend of raw

Photo by Michael Hanback

Locked on birds, exhibiting a high, classy tail, a pointer is pure beauty. Fast, wide-ranging and powerful, the breed has long been cherished by Southern bobwhite hunters. Modern foot hunters are finding the pointer versatile, capable of handling a variety of upland birds.

power and speed. A male pointer is one of the largest upland bird dogs, standing 24 inches at the shoulder and averaging 50–60 pounds. Heavier males are common; females are generally a tad smaller.

The short-coated pointer comes in many color combinations: solid white, liver and white, black and white, lemon and white, tan and white.

The pointer has a reputation for being aloof and indifferent, shunning affection. Thus, you will find more pointers in kennels than in family homes. And an amateur trainer with limited time, resources and expertise may find his hands full trying to break an independent, rambunctious pointer.

Yet there is no mistaking the breed's desire to hunt birds. Fast and powerful with seemingly unlimited stamina, running with a high, classy tail that cracks like a whip, the typically wide-ranging pointer has throughout history been considered the bobwhite quail dog in North America. This is not a one-dimensional breed, however. Keen-nosed with excellent instincts and bird sense, the pointer will hunt almost all species of upland gamebirds.

English Setter

The English setter is the epitome of beauty and style in the uplands. This is a sleek, fine-lined dog with a handsome head and face. A male English setter may average 50 to 60 pounds and stand 24 inches at the shoulder; females are often noticeably smaller.

The setter's rich, long-haired coat is colored mostly white, black and white, orange and white, lemon and white or tricolor (black, tan and white). While striking, the breed's luxuriant coat can be a problem afield; the long hair often becomes tangled with cockleburs and beggar's lice.

While some setters are aloof, most desire affection. They are comfortable in either family home or kennel. Setters are intelligent and typically respond well to training by a caring, dedicated handler.

The setter hunts beautifully, patterning a field or woodland covert gracefully, running with class and a high, feathery tail. While setters, particularly those with field-trailing ancestry, can range far and wide, many modern, close-working bloodlines have been developed for the foot hunter. This is a gundog with a keen nose and bird sense. While the setter is a classic quail, ruffed grouse and woodcock dog, it hunts all upland birds with class and heart.

Brittany

This spaniel stands, on average, 19 inches at the shoulder and weighs a compact 30 to 42 pounds. The Brittany's head and face are handsome. The breed features long, wavy-to-curly hair colored either orange and white or liver and white. Most distinctive is its short, docked tail.

The Brittany is sensitive, affectionate (to the point of craving love and attention) and gentle with children; the dog seems bred to serve as both house pet and hunting partner (though some individuals are high strung and rambunctious in the house).

Photo by Michael Hanback

The bright-eyed Brittany is a handsome, affectionate gundog. The breed's versatility—it points and retrieves most all upland birds with ease—has made it popular with hunters today.

Smart and obedient, a Brit can be effectively handled by the amateur. But use velvet hands, for the overly sensitive individual cannot accept even moderately rough training techniques.

Depending on bloodline and individual, a Brittany runs either wide and fast or close and methodical. All Brits hunt merrily, with heart and an overwhelming desire to please.

The Brittany's versatility is a boon. It is classified a "versatile" or "continental" breed, meaning it will point and retrieve game from land or water. One day, a well-trained Brit may point grouse, pheasants or quail. Next day, the spaniel will fetch with zest doves and other birds that fall on land or in marshes.

German Short-Haired Pointer

Long legs, muscular body, docked tail, head resembles the pointer's—this describes the German shorthair. Averaging 50 to 70 pounds and standing 22 to 26 inches at the shoulder, this a big gundog. And also an impressive one, with either a solid-roan or white coat splotched and ticked with liver.

The German short-haired pointer's mild-mannered temperament and trainability have popularized the breed with hunters today. The shorthair's typically slow to moderate speed, close

Photo by Leonard Lee Rue III

The German short-haired pointer typically works close and in control, making the breed a fine choice for the foot hunter.

range and methodical style afield make it a prime candidate for the foot hunter who covers small habitats for quail, grouse or woodcock.

German Wire-Haired Pointer

Hunters either love or hate the German Wire-Haired Pointer's appearance. The breed, also known as Drahthaar, features a coarse, wiry coat (grayish-white with splotches of liver), docked tail and a distinctive, heavily whiskered face. The German wirehair is typically a tad smaller than the shorthair, averaging 60 pounds and 22 to 25 inches tall at the shoulder.

Smart, sensitive, and affectionate, the wirehair makes a good house companion and is easily trained. Its short-to-medium range, keen nose and versatility (this continental breed will also actively retrieve ducks) have made the wirehair an increasingly popular choice among foot hunters today.

Flushing Breeds

English Springer Spaniel

The springer spaniel's size, beauty and disposition make the breed a favorite with hunters who wish to keep a companion in the home. The springer averages 45 pounds and stands 18 to 22 inches tall. Its liver-and-white, black-and-white or tricolor coat is rich, long and wavy. This dog has long ears with curly hair, a handsome face and a docked tail.

The gentle, affectionate springer responds well to training. Afield the spaniel hunts merrily and close to the gun. The springer is a natural for scenting, finding and flushing running birds such as pheasants and desert quail. But the breed has enjoyed a popularity boom in recent years, and can now be found in covers where once only the pointer, setter and Brittany roamed. Many foot hunters, foregoing the style and excitement of a pointing dog, have found the bouncing springer a fine woodcock and grouse dog. This spaniel is an excellent bird finder after the shot.

Labrador Retriever

Standing 22 to 25 inches at the shoulder and weighing an average of 60 to 75 pounds (females are typically smaller), the Lab is an impressive hunting dog, muscular and well-built with a short, dense coat. Solid black is the dominant color, though yellow and chocolate are not uncommon.

Despite its size, the Labrador, typically friendly and good with children, is a popular house dog. This intelligent breed is generally responsive to an amateur trainer.

America's number one waterfowl retriever is gaining favor in the uplands. The Lab possesses good speed and aggressiveness and covers grasslands and woodland coverts well. Its keen nose and instincts make the breed a natural for scent trailing and flushing birds before the gun. And rarely will you lose a downed bird with a Lab along.

Golden Retriever

The golden retriever, well-shaped and clean-lined, weighs 55 to 65 pounds and stands 21 to 24 inches at the shoulder. The golden is strikingly beautiful, with a graceful face, loving eyes and a long, rich coat colored yellow to red.

This affectionate retriever makes an excellent house companion. The best ones give the amateur trainer few disciplinary problems. In the uplands, the golden quarters nicely, if more slowly and methodically than the Labrador. And of course the golden, like the Lab, is the ultimate retriever after the shot. Many wingshooters hunt with a golden at heel as a "nonslip" retriever while a pointer or setter ranges far out front; the pointing dog finds the birds and the retriever marks, finds dead birds and brings them to hand.

Other Upland Dogs

A number of additional breeds can perform wonderfully in the uplands. You may find a field-ready Irish setter or cocker spaniel, though, in

Photo by Tom Fegely

Labrador and golden retrievers make excellent dove hunting companions. The breeds can also prove wonderfully versatile, flushing pheasants, grouse and other birds from fields, prairies and woodlands.

many cases the hunt has been bred out of these beautiful dogs. The Gordon setter, Weimaraner and Vizsla enjoy loyal followings. Less-known breeds such as the American water spaniel, Pudelpointer and pointing griffon can be excellent bird finders and retrievers, and are gaining popularity as today's foot hunters strive to find that one, all-purpose gundog.

You should consider all breeds when contemplating a gundog. Read everything you can on the breeds that seem to suit your type of hunting and lifestyle. Talk with breeders and hunters keenly familiar with the dogs that interest you. In short do your homework. Chances are you and the dog you select will get along famously, leading to many splendid days afield.

Photo by Leonard Lee Rue III

Before purchasing a gundog, consider all breeds. A dog like the Weimaraner might have a limited following among wingshooters, but its traits and hunting style might suit your needs.

Gundog Decisions

Puppy or Trained Dog?

Having selected a breed, you are now faced with choosing a puppy, started dog or fully broken bird finder.

Picking a Pup

Most bird hunters go the risky route of choosing a pup, for good reason. Puppies are fun. They are cute and cuddly, a pleasure to take home and share with the family. And training a pup is a special experience; it warms the heart to watch your dog develop from playful fur-ball to raw recruit to ultimate hunting partner.

While most puppies are purchased locally — either from a professional breeder or hunter who turns out a litter — some are ordered via mail. While it is possible to obtain an excellent gundog through a mail-order kennel, most dog-training experts recommend first seeing a puppy before you buy. These pros advocate driving hundreds of miles to a kennel if necessary to

Photos by Michael Hanback

Most breeders advise never to purchase a puppy sight unseen. Visit
a kennel and observe a litter. Hold
several pups that catch your eye.
Then thoroughly check the pedigree of both sire and dam to be
certain the puppies come from
solid hunting stock. When looking
over a litter, most hunters choose
an active, aggressive pup. But a
shy individual may bloom late and
develop into a fine hunting dog.

observe the puppies before making the great investment. The
seeing-is-believing theory applies to picking a puppy.

Once confronted with a litter of warm, cuddly, seven-week-
old puppies, resist the temptation of reaching in and pulling out
one that catches your eye before thoroughly checking the litter's
ancestry. Study the pedigree of both sire and dam.

First and foremost, be certain the puppy is from solid hunting stock. Be wary of bench or show blood in a litter, which could
possibly diminish the puppy's hunting instincts. In such breeds
as the pointer, setter and Brittany, you might well find healthy
doses of field-trialing ancestry. This represents strong hunting

and field desire, but trial dogs are bred to run far and wide. So be careful if it is a close-working gundog you desire.

If at all possible watch the litter's sire and dam hunt. Ask the breeder to turn loose the parents in a hunting situation. If he balks, be wary. What is he hiding? Have him release training birds if possible. If both sire and dam perform flawlessly on birds, your puppy comes from good stock and will have promise.

Male or female puppy? That is up to you. Male gundogs are typically larger and bolder than females, though this varies with breeds. While some claim that female dogs train easier, females can present problems when they come into heat, especially during bird season. While this can be an annoying inconvenience, most bitches can be hunted alone without incident if handled carefully.

Bold or shy pup? Most people prefer an active, aggressive individual. However, boldness does not necessarily indicate the better hunter. Many puppies are late bloomers, and a wallflower may develop into a fine gundog.

In the end, the risky business of picking a pup boils down to:

- **Locating excellent hunting stock**
- **Choosing a pup whose looks and actions catch your eye**
- **Hoping for the best**

The Started or Finished Dog

Bird hunters with limited time and training facilities, or who simply have little interest in training a puppy, may purchase a started dog. This is typically an eight-month-old pup that has been put through the initial stages of training by a breeder. A hunter may also buy an older dog, fully broken to wing and shot.

The pros of a started or finished dog include:

- Little training time or expenses.
- If you watch the dog hunt before you purchase it (by all means do!), you know what you are getting for your money.
- You can hunt the dog immediately.

The cons are:

- A started or finished dog will likely cost more.
- You miss the joy of developing a special bond with a puppy.
- You will never realize the satisfaction of hunting behind a dog you trained yourself.

Every bird hunter has individual needs. While most prefer to raise and train a puppy, others find their joy in the practicality of purchasing a started or finished gundog.

Training Basics

The ultimate goal of any training technique is to steady a gundog to wing and shot.

With a pointing breed, this entails teaching the dog to pattern within desired range, freeze promptly upon finding birds and hold until the hunter moves in to flush the game and shoot. The dog remains steady until commanded to retrieve.

A flushing dog is taught to quarter before the hunter, find birds, put them into the sky, then sit (not chase) as the hunter shoots. The dog sits until commanded to retrieve. A flushing breed may also be trained as a nonslip retriever that remains closely at heel until the hunter shoots and commands the dog to retrieve.

Photo by Leonard Lee Rue III

A variety of training theories and methods exist today, and all have one constant: dedication by handler and repetition by dog. Choose a program that strikes your fancy, then commit yourself and your dog to the routine.

In reality, most dogs trained by amateurs fall somewhere below these lofty standards. In most instances this is all right. As long as the dog performs adequately on birds, obeys the hunter and stays safely in control afield, it will provide immense pleasure to the average hunter.

Training begins the moment you bring home a seven- or eight-week-old puppy. Bonding between pup and hunter is an important foundation to any training program.

From here, there is no single right or wrong way to train an upland bird dog. A hunter may adopt a variety of training theories and methods. Each routine is unique, featuring various stages of yard training, discipline, introduction to birds and gun and retrieving.

The smart hunter who wishes to train his own puppy will review and study as many dog training books, manuals and videos as possible. He will seek the advice of professional breeders and trainers in his area. He may join a local club of dog owners/bird hunters and glean the expertise of fellow members who have trained the same breed. He will attend dog training clinics in his area.

Ultimately, he will settle into a training routine that meets his fancy and suits his leisure time and facilities. He will commit himself to that routine. If there is one constant among all the various training theories, it is dedication by the handler and repetition by the dog. These key elements will turn your dog from raw recruit to finished bird finder.

You may find you haven't the time and expertise to train your dog properly, or become frustrated with your routine. Or you may start your puppy and realize that here may be one of those once-in-a-lifetime bird dogs if given advanced teaching. In these cases, you may wish to hire a professional trainer. Sending the dog to a reputable trainer (check his references!) for weeks or months may seem expensive. But professional training could be the ticket to obtaining a well-disciplined partner that will provide fond hunting memories for years to come.

Dog Handling Afield

Handling your dog while hunting is a direct carryover from the training routine. Teach your puppy well and chances are it will obey adequately in the uplands. There are, however, two major handling techniques that will make your hunt a success rather than a frustration or even a tragedy.

Photo Courtesy Missouri Department of Conservation

Handle your dogs smartly afield. Keep them close and under control and they'll find birds, not trouble.

First, control your dog at all times. Keep it at heel or on a lead rope until you reach a bird cover, particularly when hunting small habitats in suburban areas. Allowing your dog to roam between coverts may seem good exercise for your companion, but in reality it is only an opportunity for the dog to find trouble. It may at the very least develop bad habits, such as ranging too far, hunting for itself, chasing birds or running deer. And it could get into a nearby yard, chicken lot or horse pasture, causing a tense moment between you and a landowner. Worse yet, the dog may run to a heavily traveled road and be killed.

Second, in upland covers learn to read your dog. If you sense your companion getting bored, talk to the dog, encouraging it along, getting its mind back on business. If you sense your dog beginning to quarter too far, whistle or signal it in. Read your dog's pace and watch its eyes and tail for signs of "birdiness." A few comforting commands during tense bird work may keep a young dog from making a critical mistake, offering you more shooting and solidifying the dog's ongoing field training.

CHAPTER 4

BIRD GUNS AND LOADS

S hotguns suitable for upland bird hunting come in a variety of styles. At one end of the spectrum is the plain, practical, affordable, 12-gauge pump gun. At the opposite extreme is the fine-grade, expensive, 20-gauge side-by-side. In between lies an array of semi-fancy, yet functional, autoloaders and over/unders.

Photo by Michael Hanback

Selecting the proper shotgun and tailoring loads to the birds you hunt are keys to wingshooting success.

Workings of a Shotgun

Any of these shotguns can prove excellent when matched to a wingshooter's personal taste, budget and facet of bird hunting. This chapter provides the groundwork you need to choose your optimum shotgun. Specifics include:

- **Shotgun Actions**
- **Gauges**
- **Barrels**
- **Chokes**
- **Stocks**

Then to glean the most effectiveness from your bird gun you must select the proper loads. We wind up with an overview of popular upland rounds, examining shotshell ballistics, shot sizes and pattern-testing loads for the field.

Shotgun Actions

Three types of shotguns—pump, semi-automatic and double barrel (side-by-side and over/under)—are most popular and effective for upland bird hunting in North America. The break-open single-shot and bolt-action have limited use in bird fields, and for this reason are not covered in this discussion.

Pump

Here's the pump shotgun in action. The shooter chambers a shotshell and loads two more in the magazine of a plugged shotgun. He fires the first round and chambers the second by sliding the movable fore-end rapidly back and forth. The fore-end, running on a slide, opens the action, ejects the spent shell and inserts and locks the second round. Ditto for shell number three.

The pump, featuring a relatively simple action design, is a favorite among bird hunters because of its reliability. A well-maintained pump gun rarely jams afield. And for the wingshooter who cuts his teeth on a pump, the action is quick and easy to operate. The most proficient pump gunner can shuck and fire three rounds as fast, or faster, than a shooter firing a semi-automatic.

As upland shotguns go, the pump is comparatively inexpensive. Most major firearms manufacturers build affordable pump guns today. The pump has an added advantage: Most slide-action guns, designed as bird hunting workhorses, are plain, clean-lined

Photo by Mike Strandlund

With a pump action, a hunter ejects spent shells and chambers live rounds by rapidly sliding the movable fore-end. Pumps are bird hunting workhorses, ruggedly built and rarely jamming afield.

and ruggedly built. Of course you will take care of your pump gun, but you won't be overly concerned if it becomes scarred and gouged when crossing barbed-wire fences and busting thickets and brambles.

Semi-Automatic

The semi-automatic, or autoloader, features either a gas- or recoil-operated mechanism with an internal bolt. The hunter manually chambers the first round and slips two more in the magazine. He pulls the trigger, and the gas or recoil mechanism works the bolt and automatically ejects spent shells and chambers fresh rounds.

Though simple enough to shoot, a semi-automatic shotgun is a complexity of moving internal parts. For this reason an autoloader is more prone to jam than a pump gun, especially in dusty conditions or freezing weather. A bird hunter must take great care to clean his semi-auto properly.

But the semi-automatic's positive features make it a favorite among bird hunters. Most obvious is that an autoloader provides

Photo by Michael Hanback

A semi-automatic features either a gas- or recoil-operating mechanism. Upon firing, gas or recoil works an internal bolt, ejecting spent shells and chambering new rounds. Semi-autos are easy to shoot; by simply pulling the trigger three times, a hunter can fire three quick shots at fast-rising birds.

fast, easy follow-up shots. You can concentrate on birds while simply pulling the trigger for second and third shots.

Also, a semi-auto's action is designed to lighten felt recoil. This can be a blessing when firing up to three boxes of shells at doves, or when shooting a lot of heavy "high-power" pheasant loads. Less "kick" also makes this action a good choice for young, female or slightly built wingshooters.

Many excellent semi-automatic makes and models are manufactured at home and abroad today. Most are moderately priced.

Hinge

Double-barreled shotguns come in two distinct styles, and their names say it all. The side-by-side features two horizontally aligned barrels; the over/under has a pair of vertically stacked tubes.

Both hinge-action doubles feature a lever or button on the rear of the receiver that, when pushed, breaks open the action to expose two bores. The hunter chambers two shells and closes the shotgun.

Photo by Mike Strandlund

The hinge-action over/under is popular with upland hunters today. Simply break open the shotgun and load two rounds into the exposed bores; upon firing, break the gun again to eject spent shells. With a selective trigger and two barrrels and chokes, an over/under gives you a double dose of versatility.

Upon firing, the hunter again breaks open the gun. On older models he must often remove the spent, extracted hulls. Most modern doubles feature automatic shell ejectors.

In addition to being stylish — both side-by-sides and over/unders have throughout history been considered the classic upland bird shotguns — doubles have advantages afield.

First is the presence of two barrels and chokes, hence a double dose of versatility. Most double guns feature either a single selective trigger or a selector lever on the receiver that allows you to select, and vary, which barrel/choke you fire first.

Also, double guns are inherently safe. By simply breaking open the action you know whether or not the shotgun is loaded. Also, you can easily and conveniently break the gun and remove shells when crossing a fence or creek or negotiating rugged or slick terrain. And after a slip or fall, you can easily peer down the open tubes and check for dangerous barrel obstructions like mud or snow.

Finally, doubles, by design, are generally short, lightweight and streamlined, making them fast-handling afield. Indeed, a side-by-side or over/under is custom crafted with the upland bird hunter in mind. Of course you must pay the price to own one.

Photo by Michael Hanback

The side-by-side, which features the same hinge-action design and versatility as the over/under, was once the ruling shotgun in the uplands. Modern side-by-sides are limited-production and hence expensive, but sweet-handling and forever stylish.

Fine-grade components and superior craftsmanship make doubles the most expensive upland shotguns on the market today.

Gauges

The majority of upland bird hunters are best served by a shotgun chambered for either the 12- or 20-gauge, so we will focus the following discussion on these popular gauges. While the 16- and 28-gauges and .410 bore can be effective in specialized bird hunting situations, their use and popularity are limited in the uplands of North America today.

The 12-Gauge

Here are some pros and cons of the 12-gauge.

- The 12-gauge is versatile. It is adequate for the largest, toughest pheasants and sage grouse, yet with the appropriate loads is not overkill for small, delicate birds like doves and quail. It can also be used for ducks, geese, turkey

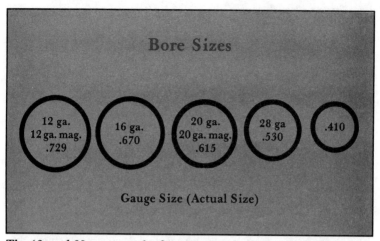

The 12- and 20-gauge are by far most popular with bird hunters. The 16- and 28-gauge can be effective, but see limited use in the uplands. The diminutive .410 is for the expert wingshooter.

and even deer, making it the obvious choice for the one-shotgun hunter.

- In theory, the 12 *should* be easier to hit with than the 20. A 2¾-inch 12-gauge "field load" has more powder and shot than a similar 20-gauge shell. This translates to added muzzle velocity, denser patterns and, in some cases, a retention of more downrange energy.
- A 12-gauge shotgun is generally heavier, more cumbersome and less maneuverable than a 20-gauge. Also, the 12 administers more recoil.

The 20-Gauge

The 20 is gaining in popularity today and is considered *the* gauge for bobwhite quail, woodcock and ruffed grouse. The 20 is the choice for anyone shooting released, close-rising birds on a preserve. With "high-power" loads a 20-gauge, in the hands of a skilled shooter, is adequate for larger birds like pheasants and western grouse and rivals the effectiveness of a 12-gauge with field loads.

Shotguns chambered for the 20-gauge are generally light-weight, streamlined and fast-handling. And administering less "kick" than the 12, the 20-gauge is an excellent choice for young or slightly built hunters.

Photo Courtesy Sturm, Ruger and Company

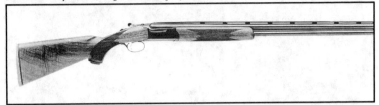

A 20-gauge like this one is lightweight, streamlined and fast-handling. With the proper loads, it is a fine choice for upland birds from woodcock to Western grouse.

Barrels

Most upland shotguns feature 26-inch barrels, and for good reason. A 26-inch tube is versatile. It is short enough to wield quickly in thick brush, yet provides an adequate sighting plane for pass-shooting doves or pigeons.

A 28-inch barrel is the maximum any upland gunner should use. While it can be cumbersome in heavy cover, it adds extra sighting dimension. This can be helpful when shooting high-flying doves or swinging on wide-flushing Western quail and pheasants late in the season.

Today, many upland shotguns come from the factory with 24-inch barrels. Following this lead, some upland hunters have had a gunsmith shorten their shotguns' barrels to 24 or 25 inches.

Indeed, short barrels are here to stay. Recent studies have shown that loss of velocity is negligible (certainly not enough to affect one's bird shooting at 20 to 40 yards) when switching from a 26- to a 24-inch barrel. And since shorter barrels lighten a shot-

Photo by Michael Hanback

Most upland bird guns have 26-inch barrels — short enough to point and swing effortlessly in thick cover, yet long enough to provide an adequate sighting plane when pass-shooting.

gun's overall weight and make it a snap to mount and point in heavy cover, they are excellent choices for the hard-walking bird hunter.

Regardless of length, every barrel on an upland shotgun should have a ventilated rib. This flat-topped rib, found on the majority of shotgun barrels manufactured today, acts as a sighting plane.

Chokes

Every shotgun barrel features a "choke"—a constriction at the muzzle that compresses shot pellets and controls the size and density of patterns. Choke specifications, from the most loosely constricted (widest spreading) to the most constricted (tightest patterning) include cylinder, skeet, improved cylinder, modified and full. Among bird hunters improved cylinder is most common. This versatile, relatively open choke patterns a variety of upland loads well from 20 to 35 yards, making it effective for most gamebirds.

Photo Courtesy Sturm, Ruger and Company

An interchangeable choke system, standard on most modern shotguns, provides the utmost in versatility. By varying loads and improved-cylinder, modified and full tubes, you can hunt all upland birds in North America with one gun.

Modified, throwing slightly tighter patterns, is effective from 25 to 40 yards. Modified is often the choice when pass-shooting high-flying doves or band-tailed pigeons. When pheasants, prairie grouse or Western quail flush wildly on windy days or late in the season, modified is a good choice. Some hunters choose to shoot full choke in these situations.

When shooting small, close-rising birds like bobwhites and woodcock, cylinder or skeet can work well. These open chokes spray pellets quickly into a wide pattern.

Years ago the upland gunner was forced to choose a shotgun with one barrel/choke and make do under a variety of situations, or spring for a double gun with two barrels and chokes. With the advent of interchangeable choke tubes, this is no longer the case.

Virtually all firearm manufacturers now offer single- or double-barrel shotguns with interchangeable choke tube systems (generally, improved cylinder, modified and full, along with wrench, are included in the purchase of a new shotgun). If you own an older gun; a number of custom gunsmiths specialize in installing choke tubes in all makes and models of hunting shotguns.

Choke tubes add versatility to the upland bird gun. You can screw in an improved cylinder at home and head afield. If you find the doves flying high or the pheasants flushing wildly, you can simply pull out your wrench and screw in a modified tube in less than 30 seconds. If bird patterns change yet again, simply tinker with tubes until you settle upon the optimum choke.

Final notes on selecting chokes. If in doubt, always choose a tight choke over an open one. Using too open a choke on birds flushing on the fringe of the choke's effectiveness can cripple game.

Choose your loads carefully. Many modern shotshells feature buffering amid copper-plated shot, which provides tighter, more uniform patterns and necessitates the selection of a slightly open choke for optimum effectiveness.

Stocks

Stocks on upland shotguns are available in two styles—with pistol grip and without, the latter commonly referred to as the straight or English stock.

Most American-made shotguns feature pistol grips, which are

Photo by Mike Strandlund

A pistol-grip stock (top) is designed to help a shooter aline and control a shotgun as he points and swings. Many wingshooters feel a straight or English stock (bottom) promotes quick, effortless pointing at fast-rising birds.

designed to help you control the gun as you point, swing and shoot. Straight stocks, popularized in Europe, are streamlined and lightweight. Some shooters feel a straight stock allows them to point the shotgun lightning fast on quickly departing birds.

Preference is basically up to you, but one fact is certain. Whether you spend $400 for a pistol-gripped autoloader or $1,500 for a straight-stocked double gun, you will shoot only as well as your shotgun fits you. Your shotgun must come up fast and point smoothly and instinctively if you are to kill birds consistently.

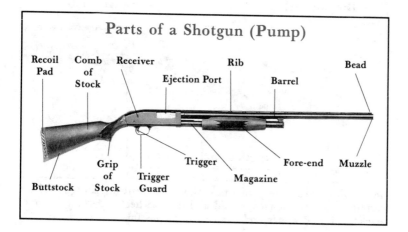

Parts of a Shotgun (Pump)

Recoil Pad · Comb of Stock · Receiver · Rib · Bead · Ejection Port · Barrel · Buttstock · Grip of Stock · Trigger Guard · Trigger · Magazine · Fore-end · Muzzle

Fit

Three major stock dimensions—length of pull, drop at comb and drop at heel—determine shotgun fit.

Length of pull is measured from the buttstock to the trigger, around 14 inches on most shotguns. But this dimension should be fine-tuned to your frame as closely as possible. Length of pull must be short enough to allow you to mount the gun smoothly without catching your shoulder or shirt, but long enough so that your head does not come down too far forward on the stock, thus throwing your natural sighting place awry.

Drop at comb is the amount of drop from the plane of the barrels to the plane of the stock. This is typically 1½ inches on factory-built guns. Since your cheek rests on the comb and your eyes line up to blot out a bird from there, this dimension is critical. Too little drop lowers your eyes, and hence you may undershoot birds. Too much drop at comb raises your eyes above the plane of the barrel, which often causes overshooting.

Drop at heel is measured from the heel (rear top) of the stock to the plane of the barrels. With most hunters the 2½ inches of drop on standard shotguns is fine, although a thick-necked, bulky shooter may need slightly more drop at heel.

The best way to attain optimum shotgun fit is to have a shotgun custom made for you. But since this is too expensive for the majority of bird hunters, you can come close by visiting your local

Photo Courtesy O.F. Mossberg and Sons, Inc.

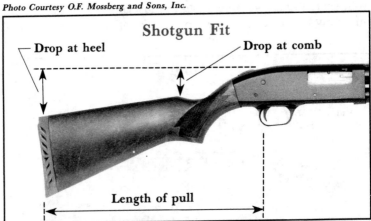

To hit birds consistently you must shoot a well-fitting shotgun. Make certain your gun's length of pull and drop at heel and comb fit your arms, neck and upper body as closely as possible.

gun shop, shouldering a shotgun and having an expert determine your critical dimensions. Then, if necessary, you can have a gunsmith shorten or lengthen your stock, or build up or shave away drop. This may seem like unnecessary expense and trouble, but you may be amazed how much better you shoot birds with a "personalized" stock tailored to your body specifications.

Selecting an Upland Shotgun

Using the previous information as a guide, you are now ready to select your optimum bird gun.

First, settle upon an action type that suits your taste and budget. Then tailor your choice to your style of hunting. Depending on which types of birds you hunt, you may desire a third shot, so a pump or autoloader is for you. But remember that a double is typically more stylish and faster handling, a fine gun, if you can afford it, for most all upland birds.

Twelve- or 20-gauge? As mentioned, the 12 is more versatile, the choice for the one-shotgun hunter. Twelves are preferred by the majority of pheasant and western grouse hunters.

If, however, you wish to specialize on small or delicate gamebirds, such as bobwhite quail, woodcock, ruffed grouse, chukar, or Hungarian partridge, the 20-gauge is perfect. And since 20-gauge are generally more lightweight and maneuverable than 12-gauge, they are pleasant to carry when trekking miles of bird cover.

Most bird hunters should choose a 26-inch barrel. It is wieldy enough for swinging quickly on flushing birds, yet provides an adequate sighting plane when leading high-flying doves. If you will typically hunt close-rising woodcock or bobwhites, a quick-pointing 24- or 25-inch barrel might serve you well.

If at all possible purchase a shotgun whose barrel or barrels feature interchangeable choke tubes, or have tubes installed in your present bird gun. Then you are ready for all bird hunting situations.

If you select a single-barrel shotgun with a fixed choke, choose the versatile improved cylinder. In a fixed-choke over/under or side-by-side choose improved and modified. These chokes will serve you best on a wide range of bird hunts.

Remember, most important is shotgun fit. Visit your local gun shop and shoulder and swing a number of shotguns. Try both pistol-gripped and straight stocks. When you settle upon the gun

Photo by Michael Hanback

Having painstakingly chosen a shotgun, oil and clean it regularly and carry it in a fleece-lined case. The gun should serve you well in the uplands for years to come.

that feels right for you, have an expert further tailor the stock dimensions to your body specs.

Having carefully chosen the upland shotgun, pattern a variety of loads and practice regularly (both topics are covered later in this chapter). Clean and oil the shotgun regularly. When traveling to the field in a vehicle, carry the gun in a soft, fleece-lined case. If traveling by airliner to a faraway bird cover, you must, by law, transport the shotgun in a hard-sided plastic or aluminum case. Take care of your bird gun and it will serve you well afield for years to come.

Upland Bird Loads

For most upland bird hunting situations, 2¾-inch shells are adequate and preferred. Three-inch loads, particularly in the 20-gauge, may be used on wild-flushing pheasants and western grouse late in the season.

Both "standard" and "high-grade" 12- and 20-gauge shells are available. Ammo manufacturers use various trademark names for these two categories of shells.

Photo by Michael Hanback

High-power 12-gauge No. 6s are a fine choice for fast-flying birds like sharp-tailed grouse.

Modern shotshell designs all have similar components:

- **Quality Primers**
- **Smokeless Powder Charges**
- **Plastic Wad Cups**
- **Hard Lead Shot**

The difference is that high-grade shotshells typically feature extra-hard or copper-plated lead shot encased in granulated buffering.

Field Versus High-Power Loads

In both standard and high-grade ammo lines you will find "field" and "high-power" loads. Field loads (you may also see them called "game" or "dove and quail" loads) have smaller powder charges and payloads than "high-brass" loads.

Typical 12-gauge field loads suitable for upland bird hunting feature 3¼ drams equivalent of powder; 20-gauge field loads have 2½. Drams equivalent, often a confusing term among hunters,

67

Photo by Michael Hanback

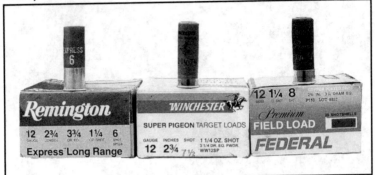

A variety of manufacturers produce top-quality high- and low-brass shotshells for upland bird hunting.

does not represent the actual amount of smokeless powder in the load.

High-power 12-gauge loads typically have 3¾ drams equivalent powder charges. High-brass 20s have around 2¾.

Both 12- and 20-gauge loads feature similar shot charges in standard and high-grade shotshell lines. In 12-gauge, field loads typically have 1 ounce of shot; in 20-gauge, ⅞-ounce. High-power 12-gauge loads have either 1⅛ or 1¼ ounces of shot; 1 ounce in the 20-gauge.

So which should you use, standard or high-grade, field or high-power loads? It depends on the type of bird hunting. All shotshells have modest velocities, with about 1,200 feet per second (fps) at the muzzle for a 12-gauge field load, and 1,150 fps for a similar 20-gauge load. Velocity is not the key element in killing upland birds cleanly. Pattern uniformity and downrange energy and penetration are most important.

Standard 12- and 20-gauge field loads will perform well in many bird hunting situations. With the proper size shot, which we will discuss in the following section, they are especially effective for doves, quail, woodcock and ruffed grouse over pointing dogs. They are also satisfactory for early-season sharptails. These standard shells are the most economical on the market today.

On many hunts high-grade field loads may kill birds more cleanly. With buffered, copper-plated shot (which does not deform in the barrel, thus no flyer pellets) these premium loads provide uniform patterns and enhanced performance at 40 yards. They are excellent choices on doves and pigeons anytime, especially when birds are flying high. In addition they are great for shooting ruffed grouse, sharptails and other western grouse.

Standard or high-grade high-power loads are popular choices for pheasants, the most difficult of upland gamebirds to kill cleanly. They may also be needed when tough sage hens and other prairie grouse flush at long ranges.

Shot Sizes

Regardless of which type of shell you shoot, you must tailor the shot size to the uplanders at hand. While it takes only four to six pellets to kill gamebirds cleanly, these pellets must be of the proper size to penetrate sufficiently.

From largest to smallest, lead shot sizes for upland birds include Number 4, 5, 6, 7½, 8 and 9 shot. The larger the shot, the less pellets in each load, but the greater the retained velocity and downrange energy. The smaller the shot, the less range, but the more expansive the pattern. Obviously, then, you should choose large shot for large gamebirds, small pellets for tiny uplanders. Also shot size should be tailored to the hunting conditions you might expect.

Shot Size and Load Chart

Shot Size	Diameter (in inches)	Shot Load Measurement in Ounces			
		1¼ oz.	1⅛ oz.	1 oz.	⅞ oz.
#4	.13	170	150	135	120
#5	.12	215	190	170	150
#6	.11	280	250	225	200
#7½	.095	440	390	350	305
#8	.09	515	460	410	360
#9	.08	730	660	585	515

Average number of pellets in popular upland bird loads.

Shot Sizes for Upland Birds

Birds	Shot Sizes
Bobwhite quail, woodcock	7½, 8, 9
Hungarian partridge, western quail	7½, 8
Ruffed, sharp-tailed grouse and prairie chickens	6, 7½
Sage grouse, other western grouse, chukar	5, 6, 7½
Pheasant	4, 5, 6, 7½
Dove	6, 7½, 8, 9

The most popular shot sizes for all-around bird hunting are 6, 7½ and 8, as evidenced by the above table that lists recommended shot sizes for all upland gamebirds.

Patterning Shotgun and Loads

Regardless of how wisely you choose an upland shotgun and loads, the only way to determine the combination's true effectiveness afield is to pattern-test. Patterning is often overlooked by wing-shooters, but patterning is critical for two reasons:

- It tells if your shotgun is shooting where you are pointing. (Remember, not all shotgun barrels necessarily do.)
- It reveals how the gun's choke is dispersing loads at a variety of bird hunting ranges.

Patterning begins with using a paper target at least 40 inches square. Draw a prominent bullseye in the center of the target. The NRA offers an interesting alternative; the Hunter Services Division sells "life-size game" targets featuring flying birds for the ultimate in realistic patterning.

Hang the target in a safe shooting zone, back up 40 yards, take a steady rest (shooting from a bench is best), hold on the bullseye and fire.

Remove the target, determine the center of the densest part of the pattern and mark it. If your shotgun is shooting where you are pointing, this mark should be on or near the bullseye or center of the bird.

Draw a perfectly symmetrical 30-inch circle around the center

NRA Life-Size Pheasant Target

Life-size pheasant targets, such as this NRA version, are valuable aids when patterning your shotgun.

mark. (The NRA targets feature pre-printed circles.) Count the pellet holes within this circle, multiply by 100 and divide by the number of pellets in each load (this information can be found in ammunition catalogs, or you can cut open a shotshell and actually count the pellets). The sum of these mathematics gives you the load's pattern percentage.

With regard to upland loads (12- or 20-gauge, all sizes of shot) firearms experts generally agree that the popular improved-cylinder choke should throw 45 to 50 percent of shot into the 30-inch circle at 40 yards. By comparison, modified chokes should pattern 55 to 60 percent.

To be effective, your loads should pattern within or near these percentages. For accurate testing, fire several shots with each load at a new target. Shoot at various ranges. Try different chokes. Then choose the loads that pattern best overall. This fine-tuning

Photo by Michael Hanback

Never go bird hunting before pattern-testing your shotgun and loads. This tells if your gun shoots precisely where you are pointing, and how its choke disperses pellets at various ranges.

of loads to chokes builds confidence in your shooting, and kills birds cleanly afield.

Special Shotgunning Considerations

Steel Shot Loads

Mandatory for all waterfowling in the United States today, steel shot may be required for some upland bird hunters in various regions and on select state and federal lands. Other hunters may simply wish to test the effectiveness of steel shot on close-rising birds.

If so, No. 6 steel is the best choice on the market today. A 1¼-ounce load has about 400 steel pellets, approximately 120 more pellets than a comparable lead load. The steel's muzzle velocity is approximately 1,350 fps, some 300 fps faster than No. 6 lead. This is mainly because steel pellets are lighter than lead. While No. 6 steel may pattern densely at short range, its velocity falls off sharply at 30 to 35 yards. Take this into consideration and restrict shots accordingly when shooting steel.

Muzzleloading for Upland Birds

Gunning upland gamebirds with an authentic or a replica muzzleloading shotgun has seen a recent resurgence of interest. If you have access to an original muzzleloading shotgun, be sure to have it checked out by a qualified black powder gunsmith before heading afield.

For more information on how to bird hunt with a muzzleloader, see the NRA Hunter Skills Series book, *Muzzleloader Hunting* and the NRA Basic Firearms Education manual, *The Muzzleloading Shotgun Handbook*.

Photo by Russ Carpenter

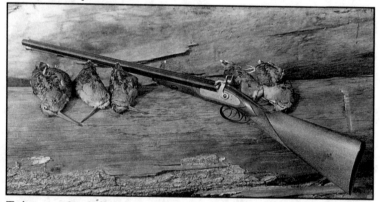

To increase the challenge, the hunter may consider using a muzzleloading shotgun for upland birds.

CHAPTER 5

GUNNING UPLAND BIRDS

Over the years, with the specialization of bird hunting and the advent of such fine clay target games as international skeet and sporting clays, many advanced, innovative wingshooting theories have been developed. Most have merit, but can be confusing and difficult to perfect for the average sportsman. Not to worry. The upland hunter, after understanding the

Photos by Wicker Bill

Adopting solid shooting fundamentals, practicing regularly, then bird hunting as much as possible will help you become a crack wingshot.

fundamentals of shotgunning and using a well-fitting shotgun and proper loads, can kill birds consistently by employing three simple, time-tested techniques:

- **Snap Shooting**
- **Swing Through**
- **Sustained Lead**

The Fundamentals

The best way to learn wingshooting is to build a solid foundation of shotgun-handling skills and then, through field experience, learn to compute instantly and subconsciously all the factors that go into making a shot. These fundamentals include the following:

1) **Stance**
2) **Gun-Ready Position**
3) **Swing to Target**
4) **Trigger Pull**
5) **Follow-Through**

Photo by Mike Strandlund

These steps are combined and refined for each specific situation to allow you to compensate for variations in shooting conditions, speed, angle, distance, and type of flight.

Dominant Eye

Before you can learn these wingshooting fundamentals, you must decide whether to shoot right- or left-handed. To do this, determine your dominant eye — the eye that sees the "strongest" image and the one you want to align with the bead and the target.

Successful wingshooting begins with proper footwork, stance and gun-mounting form. Practice these fundamentals until they become natural links in your shotgunning technique.

Good Form

Whether snap shooting or leading, effective upland gunning begins with proper form. Solid fundamental technique balances your body; promotes smooth shotgun mounting, pointing and swinging; then provides effortless follow through.

For years experts have preached to stand with your feet shoulder-width apart. If this feels comfortable, do it. Today, however, many wingshooting instructors suggest that you stand with your heels as closely together as possible while maintaining good balance. The theory is that a narrow stance allows you to pivot freely when turning or swinging on birds.

If you're a right-handed shooter, place your left foot slightly forward, pointing toward the anticipated line of fire. Bend your knees slightly. Square your hips and upper body to the direction you plan to shoot.

Grasp the shotgun firmly at its stock and lightly at its fore-end. Hold the gun comfortably perpendicular to your body, pointing in the general direction you plan to shoot. Many hunters mistakenly hold their shotguns parallel across their chests; this seriously inhibits their ability to get on birds quickly and effortlessly. Hold the butt of the shotgun from waist high to just below the underarm — whichever feels comfortable for you. The muzzle should be at or slightly below eye level. This puts both the shotgun muzzle and the flushing bird in your natural line of sight, allowing you to focus, point and shoot in one smooth, instinctive motion.

Determining Lead

A common mistake by beginning shotgunners is to shoot where the target is, rather than where it will be when the pellets arrive. They often fail to realize that it takes significant time for the shot to get there. Several factors affect lead, including:

- **Distance Between Shooter and Target**
- **Target Speed**
- **Reaction, Lock and Ignition Times**
- **Shot Velocity**
- **Angle of Target Flight**
- **Muzzle Swing Speed**

The most significant factors are distance and the speeds of the target and shot. For example, consider a 35-yard crossing shot on a mourning dove flying 40 miles per hour. The dove's speed translates to about 60 feet per second, compared with the average velocity of the shot at 1,000 feet per second. It will take your shot about one-tenth of a second to travel those 35 yards to the dove. In that same tenth of a second, the dove will have traveled six feet. To center the dove in the pattern, you will have to lead it by six feet, all other things being equal.

Time Delays in Shooting

| Follow-thru | Shot Travel | Mechanical Delay | Shooter's Reaction Time | Target Travel |

—DOUG PIFER

A shotgunner must adjust his lead to compensate for time and distance factors affecting target and pattern. He must instantly and subconsciously compute target speed and angle, shooter reaction time, mechanical delay, shot travel time and the speed of follow through.

But remember, all things aren't always equal. There is also the angle of flight—if the dove is flying a bit toward or away from you, its lateral speed is reduced, and your lead must change correspondingly. Forward allowance (or lead) should be cut in half if the target is flying half as fast, is twice as close or is angling at 45 degrees toward or away from you. Keep in mind reaction time—the time lapse between the instant your brain says, "pull the trigger" and you actually do pull the trigger. There is also the less significant lock time (time for your gun's mechanism to work) and ignition time (time it takes for the primer to go off, the powder to burn and the pellets to travel down the barrel). These time lapses usually total about one-fifth of a second.

Obviously this is all too much to think about as you try to shoot a passing mourning dove. You have to learn through practice to calculate lead instantly, subconsciously. You must also take into consideration the type of swing you use.

Shooting Techniques

Snap Shooting

Snap shooting relies on your instincts, hand-eye coordination and athletic ability. This natural shooting technique is excellent for most upland bird hunting situations, especially when birds like quail and grouse flush close and fly straightaway.

Photo Courtesy Outdoor Oklahoma

Snap shooting relies on your reflexes, hand-eye coordination and athletic ability. This instinctive technique is excellent for many bird hunting situations, such as when bobwhites whir up and fly straightaway.

Here's a typical snap-shooting scenario. You slip in behind a pointing dog, your shooting form immaculate, and a covey of bobwhites whirs away. First you focus on a single bird. Then you raise your shotgun smoothly to your check and lean slightly forward until your shoulder contacts the buttstock (never jerk the buttstock back to meet the shoulder). Resist the urge to drop your head sharply into the shotgun's comb. Simply raise the gun until it meets your cheek. This is why proper drop at comb on your gun is critical.

During the gun-mounting process you have continued to focus upon the bird while instinctively slipping off the safety. Never push off the safety prior to birds flushing; it is extremely dangerous. Now, the instant your shoulder taps the buttstock, and when the straightaway target sits "on top" of your sighting plane, pull the trigger. On an angling or crossing bird you point and fire at a spot where your mind instinctively tells you bird and shot pattern will meet.

In short, focus, point and fire. Your shotgun becomes a natural extension of your body. Depending solely on hand-eye coordination, reflexes and natural ability, there is little thinking to this technique. And this should benefit most upland gunners, since thinking too much about lead, range and crossing angles often gets shooters in trouble afield.

Swing Through

There are times, of course, when you must think about leading upland birds. Such as when pass-shooting doves or band-tailed pigeons. Or when pheasants or sharptails fly between fields and roosts in late afternoon. Or when ringnecks or western quail flush wide and fly at difficult, long-range crossing angles. In these instances one of two related swing and lead shooting methods must be employed.

The swing-through technique is popular with many upland hunters because it is the most natural and easiest to master. It has an added advantage—it encourages the shooter to keep the shotgun's muzzle swinging as he or she follows through, critical to success in most wingshooting situations.

Using swing-through, the shooter focuses on the bird, swings the muzzle smoothly from behind and past the target, fires when the bead covers target and then follows through, continuously swinging. The shooter is not estimating lead, but leading through timing the trigger pull. For this reason there must be no hesitation in swing speed or trigger pull.

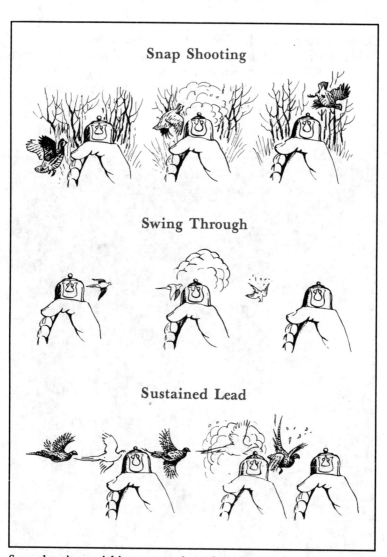

Snap Shooting

Swing Through

Sustained Lead

Snap shooting—picking a spot where the pellet charge and target will intersect—is often best on suddenly flushed game or where shots must be threaded through timber. The swing-through can be effective anytime substantial lead is necessary—such as when pass-shooting doves or pigeons. The hunter focuses on the bird, swings the shotgun's muzzle smoothly from behind and past the target, fires when the lead appears correct, then continues swinging as he follows through. With sustained lead, the shooter maintains a constant forward allowance in front of his target, firing when he feels his swing and lead are right.

Sustained Lead

For the highest flying doves or pigeons, the sustained-lead method can be effective. The shooter estimates lead and swings well ahead of the bird. Sustaining your swing, you fire when you feel you've locked into the proper lead. Because the shotgun's muzzle is not moving as fast as in the swing-through technique, more lead is essential with this method.

Photo by Bob Miles, Arizona Game and Fish Department

When hunting in rough terrain, the importance of proper shooting form and technique becomes critical to the success of the hunter.

Pheasant Vital Areas

—DOUG PIFER—

The vital zone on upland gamebirds is much smaller than the bird appears. Usually at least three or four hits—within the energy range of the pellet—are needed to bring the game down immediately.

Practice Techniques

Before heading afield, develop a comfortable, well-balanced shooting stance and practice mounting and swinging your unloaded shotgun over and over until the process becomes natural. Then, shooting clay targets year-round will sharpen your eye. Skeet and trap can be excellent, if structured, practice. Sporting clays, the new rage that simulates field gunning, is the ultimate tune-up drill. Shooting at a variety of clay birds whistling low through trees and floating high overhead is a fine way to hone your snap-shooting and swing-and-lead techniques.

When to Shoot

While some upland birds are shot at 15 to 25 paces, there are occasions when birds flush or cross at 25 to 40 yards and beyond. Generally speaking, to kill birds consistently and reduce crippling loses, restrict your shooting to 40 yards or less.

83

NRA Staff Photo

Shooting skeet or trap year-round will sharpen your shooting eye. Getting into sporting clays, shooting targets that whistle through trees and zip overhead at various angles, is the ultimate way to hone your snap-shooting and swing-and-lead techniques.

As range increases, lead becomes critical, so all hunters should hone their range-estimating skills.

This can be difficult, since upland birds come in an array of sizes and fly at various speeds and angles. The best way to tune range estimation is to hunt a lot, burning into your mind the sight picture of birds at various distances.

But there are pre-hunt techniques that can help. Such as setting a dove decoy or dead quail or grouse in a tree and stepping off 10, 20, 30 and 40 yards. From these ranges, shoulder, point and swing your unloaded shotgun at and through the "bird" over and over. Then approach the "bird" from various unknown yardages and point and swing your shotgun. Estimate the range and step it off to see how effective you are becoming at judging distances. With practice, you will print a variety of sight pictures into your mind, which will lead to more cleanly folded birds afield.

Part II
How to Hunt Upland Birds

Photo by Leonard Lee Rue III

CHAPTER 6

DOVES

O n a hot, humid, hazy afternoon in early September, a party of 20 camouflaged hunters, carrying shotguns, ammo boxes, stools and buckets, sets out across a shimmering sea of cut corn. At the heels of a couple of hunters tag Brittanies and Labradors.

The hunters fan out, taking stands along every ditch, fence row and tree line in sight, strategically encircling the grainfield. They then sit quietly atop their stools and buckets, waiting.

In late afternoon, mourning doves begin trickling into the field. Shotguns pop sporadically. A half-hour later the sky is a canvas of gray as hundreds of doves twist, dive and sweep into the field for their afternoon feeding. Shotguns boom simultaneously, continuously. Hunters yell to their partners, "Mark ... Over your head ... Nice shot!" Labs and Brits work overtime fetching birds for their handlers.

Then all is silent again; the evening flight ends as abruptly as it began. The party of hunters gathers back at their vehicles, sipping ice water and tea, wiping down their still-warm shotgun barrels, laughing and reliving their exciting day afield.

Photo by Leonard Lee Rue III

Mourning doves usher in bird season with a bang each September. Abundant, fast-flying and delicious on the table, the sporty little gamebirds are favorites of millions of wingshooters across North America.

Such is the nature of dove hunting in North America. When field conditions are right and the birds are in, this zesty September gunning ushers in fall hunting season with a bang. It is a time when novice hunters and veterans, youngsters and parents alike, gather to enjoy a fine afternoon of camaraderie, wingshooting and dog work. And later that evening the dove breasts barbecued on an outdoor grill are superb!

Range

The mourning dove is the most widespread sporting bird in North America today. It inhabits in varying numbers, depending upon the time of year and the weather, all of the contiguous United

Source: **Management of Migratory Shore and Upland Game Birds,** *Sanderson (Editor)*

Range of Mourning Dove

States. While doves can be found summering in the southern portions of most Canadian provinces, even up into the panhandle of Alaska, the warm-weather birds migrate south to winter in favorable climes across the United States and Mexico.

The white-winged dove is also of interest to upland bird hunters, but has a limited range in the United States. White-wings are desert birds, found in southernmost Texas, New Mexico, Arizona and California along the Mexican border.

Biology and Behavior

Photo by Maslowski

The mourning dove, *Zenaidura macroura*, is a sleek, delicate gamebird with a streamlined body and small head. It weighs three to six ounces and is 10 to 12 inches long, including its pointed tail.

Both male and female mourning doves are cloaked with gray-brown backs and wings and beige undersides. In sunlight, the birds' iridescent feathers radiate a pinkish-bluish sheen. Their wings are dotted with black; there is also a distinctive black spot near each ear.

Sleek and streamlined, the mourning dove weighs three to six ounces and is 10 to 12 inches long, including its pointed tail.

Mourning doves are prolific. Depending on location, pairs nest in brush, trees and, at times, on the ground from spring through autumn. They rear two to four broods of two with an incubation period of 13 to 15 days. Yet the species suffers a staggeringly high mortality rate due to disease, predation and bad weather. While this fluctuating life-death scenario makes estimating dove numbers complex, biologists believe some half a billion little gray birds wing across North America each year.

Photo Courtesy Arizona Game and Fish Department

Photo by Leonard Lee Rue III

Mourning doves are prolific, breeding spring through autumn in various corners of North America. Female doves nest in trees and rear two to four broods of two each year.

While millions of mourning doves migrate (thus the species falls under federal migratory bird hunting regulations), droves of resident birds live and breed year-round in contiguous states with favorable climates. The mourning dove is an adaptable gamebird capable of inhabiting most any open, broken habitat, from Western prairies and deserts to Midwestern farms, from Eastern shores to Southern mixed hardwoods and coastal plains.

Doves typically feed twice a day, flying to an "idle" natural field or harvested grainfield in early morning and late afternoon. There the birds pick the fallen seeds of ragweed and other flora, or feed heavily upon spilled corn, soybeans, sunflowers, milo, wheat and other grains. Doves generally water after feeding.

Though the mourning dove coos softly during mating time, most hunters may not be aware of it. What hunters will hear, however, is the whistling of dove wings, for this gamebird's twisting, acrobatic flight is legendary. Doves have been clocked at over 60 miles per hour, and their small, streamlined bodies give the illusion of even greater speed.

Photo by George Andrejko, Arizona Game and Fish Department

White-winged doves inhabit arid desert habitat in the Southwestern United States. Hunters should locate watering areas, such as rivers and livestock tanks, where large numbers of these birds concentrate.

91

The southwestern white-winged dove, *Zenaida asiatica*, is easily distinguished in flight by its white wing patches. The whitewing is about 12 inches long, weighs several ounces more than the mourning dove and is grayish-brown overall. Its squared, white-tipped tail is another distinctive feature.

Whitewings feed primarily on the fallen seeds of a variety of desert weeds. In their arid environment, these doves are heavily dependent on water and often fly great distances to drink in morning and afternoon.

Source: **Management of Migratory Shore and Upland Game Birds,** *Sanderson (Editor)*

Range of White-winged Dove

Dove Hunting Tactics

The Art of Field Shooting

The most common and productive dove hunting method across North America is to take a stand along a harvested grainfield in September and gun birds as they pour in to feed upon left-over corn, milo, wheat, sunflowers or soybeans.

Successful hunting begins with finding a "hot" dove field. First the doves must find a field. In areas where few grainfields are cut in early September—when the local crops are either late to ripen or the weather is too rainy for farmers to get tractors and combines into the muddy fields—resident doves will quickly locate and use the first fields harvested. But in expansive farming country where thousands of acres of grain may be harvested at once and feed is plentiful, it may take doves a week or more to begin using a field where you plan to hunt.

Photo by Bob Miles, Arizona Game and Fish Department

Shooters fanning out across a field, setting up strategically in corners and fence rows, then gunning birds as they wing in to feed is the most common method of dove hunting. Doves come in droves or small flocks to pick seeds or harvested grain morning and evening.

So it is up to you to find the hottest dove field in your area. One way is to ride back roads in early September, noting which fields have been cut, and observing which are in the process of being harvested. Drive around morning and evening if possible, when doves are actively feeding. With the naked eye or binoculars search overhead power lines and trees on the edges of cut fields; doves will perch here to survey the area before bombing in to feed. Of course look for doves sweeping into or sitting and feeding in a field.

Once doves find a field, they generally feed there early each morning, and then shooting can be excellent. Be advised, however, that many states, feeling a need to allow local doves one peaceful feeding per day, begin hunting hours at noon. Read your hunting regulations carefully before planning a morning hunt.

After this early feeding, doves loaf in nearby trees during the typically hot midday hours. Come 3:00 or 4:00 p.m. the birds bomb the field for their major afternoon feeding. On cool, cloudy, drizzly early-autumn afternoons, the doves may return earlier, flocking to fields to feed as early as 1:00 p.m.

Regardless of whether you plan to hunt the morning or evening feeding, you should arrive early at the dove field, for flights can be fleeting. In areas where feed is plentiful, the frenzied flying may last an hour or less.

Arriving early at a field offers an added advantage. You'll get first crack at prime dove stands. While most any stand can produce some shooting when doves are actively using a field, the following posts will typically offer the hottest gunning.

First is a tree or dead snag brushed with weeds in or near the center of a cut grainfield. Foremost, this stand offers excellent visibility, a 360-degree view of flying doves. And doves often glide into such structure to sit and study the field below. Hide in the hay or weeds encircling the tree or snag and you will glean easy incoming shots.

A low, overgrown ditch coursing through a cut grainfield is also an excellent spot to stand for doves. Well-hidden in tall grass or weeds, you can often enjoy fine gunning at doves sweeping in low to feed.

A low, brushy fence line rimming a grainfield is a popular and strategic spot for a dove stand. In big fields, you should scout if possible, patterning the direction from which the majority of doves are entering the shooting ground. Then you can set up

Gunning A Dove Field

By boxing a field, a hunting party can keep incoming doves swirling, providing shooting for everyone. Prime stands include brushy fence rows, gaps in tree lines, overgrown ditches and dead snags. For safety, set up 100 yards from the nearest hunter and determine safe lines of fire. Note: It may be illegal to hunt in unharvested croplands.

along the fence, strategically in the flight path, and enjoy consistently hot shooting.

When hunting a grainfield, much of the time you must stand backed up to a tree line or block of still-standing crops. You can easily cover 180 degrees out front, but you'll be hunting blind when doves wing in from behind. To counter this, arrange a line of communication with a partner hunting across the field from you. When he or she sees doves flashing in behind you, your partner shouts, "Mark!" or "Over your head!" You return the favor. With this notice, you can turn, back 10 yards out into the field and snap shoot doves that whip suddenly overhead.

Another solution is to set up in a gap in a tree line where you have a sliver of an opening through which to catch a glimpse of doves boring in from behind. And hunt a natural pass if you can find it, a low, wide opening in tall trees. Such a tunnel naturally funnels doves, offering excellent shooting if you are set up nearby.

How many hunters should fill these field stands? It depends on the dimensions of the field, of course, but plan on enough guns along the edges (spaced at least 100 yards apart for safe shooting) to box the field, with a hunter or two crouched safely in the middle if possible. Such a setup covers a field strategically. The gunning keeps incoming doves swirling, offering shooting for everyone.

If your party over-guns a field early in the season, perhaps more than twice a week, doves will leave for greener pastures. This is particularly true if there are a number of freshly cut fields in the vicinity. Doves also naturally shun a field as more local crops are harvested. This is the time to scout for fresher, more active dove fields.

Dove hunting needn't be confined to harvested grainfields. Hunting over fields of natural dove feed, such as ragweed, foxtail, doveweed and many other mixed weeds, can be effective. This mode of hunting is more spotty than grainfield hunting. Scouting local doves to find pockets where they are feeding is critical to success. Hunting wild fields can be especially effective for both mourning and white-winged doves out West.

Don't rule out dove hunting near or over a gravel pit or stone quarry. Abandoned dirt roads and dried up creek bottoms offer good shooting too.

Hunting Roosts

Fine early-evening shooting can be had by locating prime dove roosts. Doves typically roost in small, bushy trees, such as cedars, low-growing pines and scrub oak. Dead snags along a creek or river bottom are also prime roosts. Search for these roosts within a mile or so of fields where doves are actively feeding.

While doves are gregarious — hundreds, even thousands, may converge upon a prime feeding area — the birds often flock loosely when flying to roosts. Scattered concentrations of doves may gather in a number of roosts located across the countryside. You should scout several bands of cedars and pines and a couple of creek bottoms in your area, watching an hour or so before dusk to see which roosts doves are using most heavily.

Then set up, well hidden, in early evening and pass-shoot mourning doves or whitewings as they stream from fields to roost. Often flocks of doves will come at once. The shooting will be fast and furious, but over in 10 minutes. Sometimes birds will

Photo by Leonard Lee Rue III

Doves typically roost in scrub oak, cedar, pine and dead trees lining a creek bottom. For the hottest action, hunt a roost near a field where birds are actively feeding.

trickle in in pairs and small flocks. Fine gunning can then be enjoyed for an hour or more.

Hunting Water Holes

Doves typically water at least once a day, gathering morning or afternoon at ponds, stock tanks, streams, creeks or rivers located near feeding and roosting areas.

In areas where water is limited, such as in the arid West and Southwest, water-hole shooting is most effective. In the desert it is easy to scout scattered ponds, tanks and streams and discover where and when large concentrations of mourning and white-winged doves flock to drink.

The optimum setup is to arrive early at the water hole and conceal yourself along the fringe. When the doves arrive, they can be shot like ducks as they glide in to drink. When hunting a large pond or meandering stream, a dozen dove decoys placed

Hunting A Water Hole

—DOUG PIFER

When hunting over a large pond or stream, setting a few dove decoys in a dead snag or along a wire fence helps pull birds your way.

in a nearby snag or atop a wire fence may help pull birds over the section of water you are covering.

Late-Season Hunting

By the end of September, doves are forgotten game for most upland bird hunters, whose interests turn to upcoming quail, pheasant and grouse seasons. While many dove seasons have closed by October, some states offer late seasons that extend into December in some areas. Challenging shooting, mostly for wary migratory doves pushed down from the north by cold weather, can be experienced by the hardy dove hunter.

This is tough, solitary sport that calls for unique tactics. You will never find crowds of hunters covering a grainfield as they

Photo by Michael Hanback

Late in the season, patterning small flocks of doves as they wing in to feed and jump-shooting field edges are best ways to score.

did in September. That is all right, because you will not find huge dove concentrations either. However, you may well find a healthy number of northern doves flocking to a field, even if it was cut several months before.

Pattern the late arrivers as they flock to a feeding area. Scouting for that premium dove stand is crucial to late-season success. With a limited number of birds around and no other hunters to keep them moving, you must be at precisely the right place at the right feeding time to scratch down several birds.

This is also a prime time to jump-shoot doves. While jump-shooting can be effective early in the season, mainly during mid-day when the doves are inactive and resting, this technique seems tailor-made for late-season hunting.

After scouting and finding doves, you can jump-shoot one of two ways. Either walk the edges of a field, shooting at doves that flush from trees or bushy fringes, or try sneaking up on birds feeding in a field. Either way you face difficult shooting. Having been hunted for several months, the doves are wary and will likely flush wildly. Switching from improved cylinder choke to modified or full is often the key to bagging a couple of birds.

Final Considerations

As upland bird hunting goes, dove shooting is unique. Most of the time you will be stand-hunting, waiting well-concealed for doves to come to you rather than walking and flushing birds. Therefore, the sport requires several special gear and gundog considerations.

First, gear. Camouflage, green or khaki clothing is a must for concealing yourself from sharp-eyed doves.

Whether shooting a field, roost or water hole, you should always carry a stool or bucket to sit on. Not only will this make you more comfortable as you wait for doves to fly, it will enhance your shooting. Struggling up from a crouching or kneeling position to shoot at doves rocketing overhead is awkward. Rising effortlessly from a stool or bucket promotes good stance and shooting form.

When the birds are in, a dove hunter may burn one, two or more boxes of shells. Small foam or rubber ear plugs will protect your hearing and should be used for all shooting.

As mentioned, dove decoys can be helpful, and not only in water-hole shooting. Scattering a dozen or more gray, full-bodied decoys or silhouettes along a wire fence or high in a snag near your field stand may pull doves in your direction.

As for dogs, since the sport requires no pointing or flushing, you will do best with a retriever or versatile breed *if* your dog will retrieve doves. Some dogs dislike the feel and taste of loose dove feathers, while others readily fetch the gray birds.

The tangible benefits of dove hunting, for both you and gundog, are two-fold:

- Little gray doves dropped in woods, standing crops, heavy brush or fields of ragweed can be difficult to locate on your own; a dog will conserve game by helping you mark and find all birds.
- The early September work on game is unmatched for polishing the retrieving skills of a Lab, golden, Brittany or German shorthair; it is excellent, too, for sharpening your dog-handling commands.

Photo by Bob Miles, Arizona Game and Fish Department

A Lab can help you find little gray doves dropped in thick brush, and the early-season work primes the dog for duck season.

Where to Go

America's most numerous and widespread upland gamebird, the mourning dove is hunted in most every corner of the country (though a few states classify the dove as a songbird and have no open season). Of the 50 million mourning doves harvested by hunters each year, half are believed shot in the Coastal Plain, that huge arc of states from southern New England southwest to southern Texas. Within this arc all the Deep South states traditionally offer top-notch dove hunting.

The desert Southwest is a dove hunting hot spot for both mourning and white-winged doves. Any hunter interested in traveling to the dove shoot of a lifetime should consider Mexico, where many commercial outfitters and lodges offer excellent gunning for huge concentrations of whitewings and other Mexican dove species.

CHAPTER 7

BOBWHITE QUAIL

A merica's quail. This best describes the bobwhite, the little russet bird who has, over time, stolen the hearts of upland hunters across the United States. Throughout history no other species has provided such tradition-rich, yet diversified, gunning. Whether rising from broomsedge on a sprawling southern plantation, with tweed-coated sportsmen on horseback in hot pursuit, or whirring from a brushy edge before the typical foot hunter in tattered canvas, the bobwhite has provided scintillating wingshooting for decades.

Today, the bobwhite quail, delicately beautiful and a challenging target, continues to be a favorite of upland gunners. Yet the pursuit of quail is markedly different than it was years ago. While bobwhite numbers are slowly rebuilding in some states, they are but a remnant of what they once were in many parts of North America. Why? Loss of quail habitat, due to a shift to clean-farming practices and development, is the chief culprit.

The "modern" bobwhite, pushed into limited new habitats and fighting for survival, is a new breed of gamebird. While once quail fed in open fields for hours morning

Photo by James M. Norine

For decades the bobwhite, delicately beautiful and a challenging target, has been a favorite of upland gunners.

Photo by Maslowski

Look for bobwhites in thick habitat today — along brushy fence rows and field edges, amid honeysuckle tangles, even deep in woodlands.

and afternoon, the birds now often inhabit the nastiest cover available, venturing only out to edges on short feeding forays. Where once bobwhites held predictably in the semi-open for pointing dogs, now they are spooky, often running and flushing wildly into thick brush and woodlands. Where once flushed birds sailed down within easy sight of the hunter, singles now often fly out of the country.

It is obvious, then, that the quail hunter, if he or she expects consistent success, needs specialized techniques today. After first examining the biology and behavior of this "new-breed" bobwhite, this chapter focuses on timely tactics that should produce successful wild quail gunning all season long.

Range

The bobwhite quail, *Colinus virginianus*, is primarily a bird of the Eastern United States. It ranges from Florida north to southern New England; from the Atlantic Coast west to eastern New Mexico and Wyoming; and from southern Texas north to southern

Source: Grouse and Quails of North America, *Johnsgard*

Range of Bobwhite Quail

Minnesota. Introduced into Idaho, Washington and Oregon, bobwhites exist in scattered pockets.

Biology and Behavior

Bobwhites are eight to 10 inches long and weigh around seven ounces. Both hens and cocks are russet-brown overall with mottled, white-flecked breasts. Males are easily distinguished by white and black stripes upon their faces; females have buff and brown facial markings.

Modern bobwhite habitat consists of brushy fence rows, overgrown fields and ditches, honeysuckle tangles and the thick fringes of croplands. In their Western range, the birds are found in grasslands and brush-laced valleys, canyons and river bottoms. While bobwhites have traditionally used the edges of pines and hardwoods, today they often live deep in the woods. Clearcuts and burns provide excellent habitat.

Bobwhites feed after sunrise, gleaning weed seeds, legumes, pine seeds, berries, acorns and other natural foods. Spilled corn and other grains are preferred. Quail feed heavily on grasshoppers, mosquitoes and other insects during spring and summer. After the morning feeding, quail loaf in nearby security cover, then move out to feed again in late afternoon.

The bobwhite is monogamous, meaning each cock breeds only one hen each spring. In a ground nest, hens lay 14 to 16 buff-colored eggs that hatch in about 24 days. If the initial spring nesting attempt is disrupted by farming equipment, inclement weather or predators, there is often a second laying of eggs.

Photo by Maslowski

A covey of bobwhites roosts on the ground in a close-knit circle. With heads pointed outward, the quail can detect a predator slipping in from any angle.

Bobwhites are gregarious most of the year, gathering in typical coveys of 10 to 15 birds. Coveys roost on the ground in a distinctive circle. Tails inward and bodies touching, heat is transmitted throughout the covey on cold nights. Heads pointing outward, the birds scan 360 degrees for predators.

Photo by Maslowski

The quail's "bob-white" call is distinctive in springtime, when cock birds establish territories. Single birds utter a "whoo-hee-whoo" assembly call when a covey is scattered.

When flushed, bobwhites whir up on tiny, curved wings and fly low to moderately high at speeds up to 30 mph. Singles may glide 100 to 300 yards (often farther today) before sitting down.

The quail's "bob-white, bob-bob-white" call is distinctive, especially in springtime when cock birds are establishing and defining their territories. The birds also utter a "whoo-hee-whoo" assembly call when a covey is scattered.

Bobwhite Hunting Tactics

Finding the Edge

The bobwhite quail has always been an edge bird, feeding near the fringes of fields and loafing in security cover during the day. Brushy draws, ditches and fence rows rimming open weed fields

The Quail Edge

DOUG PIFER

Today's "new-breed" bobwhites often inhabit the nastiest, most secluded edge cover they can find. (1) Look for coveys where thick evergreens border field and fence lines, (2 and 3) check the edges of second-growth saplings, (4) hunt the brush-laced fringes of clearcuts, (5) burns, and (6) swamps and creeks.

or harvested croplands have always been excellent edges in which to find quail, and this still holds true.

There are, however, new edges you should hunt today. When scouting a piece of country that should hold a covey or two of bobwhites, seek out the most secluded edge, however inconspicuous, you can find. This may be a row of cedars splitting an overgrown weed field. Or thick pines rimming hardwoods. Or second-growth saplings bordering a stand of mature hardwoods. In short, look for the densest, nastiest, most diversified edge cover in the area—chances are you will find bobwhites there.

Remember, too, that quail in many areas, particularly where broken-field habitat is shrinking or hunting pressure is keen, have been pushed deeper into forests. Here the birds must adapt their daily routine to their new woodland habitat. Prime, food-rich edges to hunt include the fringes of clearcuts, burns and meadows surrounded by hardwoods. Brushy swamp bottoms laced with honeysuckle are prime security covers to check in midday, as are the weedy edges of creeks and streams.

To find wild quail in today's nasty edge cover, success depends heavily on a well-trained gundog. Pointing breeds are preferred, both for pinning birds and providing sporty wingshooting. A minority of modern quail hunters use flushing breeds to roust quail from the densest edge. If you intend to hunt bobwhites regularly, invest in a gundog or hunt over a partner's dogs. You will hunt effectively and enjoy the experience immensely.

Photo by Michael Hanback

A well-trained pointing dog is invaluable for pinning quail in thick cover.

Early-Season Techniques

Hunting bobwhites in October or November, depending upon when the season opens in your area, has pros and cons.

Many quail are still in family groups through the first winter. At times, two families are often found together, ballooning coveys

Photo by Michael Hanback

During midday, a fine place to find loafing quail is around a crumbling homestead rimmed with briars and brush.

to 25 to 30 birds. Birds of the year, by now full grown, have never been hunted and hold well for a pointing dog.

Not yet shriveled and weakened by heavy autumn frosts, food and cover are abundant. Bobwhites, scattered over the countryside in a variety of habitats, can be difficult to pinpoint. In many areas it is hot and dry, making scenting conditions tough for the keenest nosed pointer, setter, shorthair or Brittany.

When hunting early in the season, arrive at the quail cover at the crack of dawn. With food plentiful, coveys may linger feeding only a few minutes before retreating to security cover, where they can glean seeds and leaves while loafing. Covering a lot of edge early is the best way to find feeding quail.

Early in the morning, listen for quail. Coveys often whistle when moving out to feed. And if the covey was scattered by a predator in the night, the singles will be assembly calling frantically. You can blow a small, round, single-holed quail call to elicit response. Hearing whistling quail obviously tells you where to concentrate your hunting.

When hunting midday, you must hunt the densest security cover you can find, as the birds will be laying low. A tip here.

Don't make the mistake of busting headlong into thick, head-high cover; let your dogs scour the thickets while you walk through a sliver of opening. If you become entangled in dense cover, it will be nearly impossible to shoot if a covey erupts. And it will be difficult to mark the singles.

In late afternoon, move back to the fringes, hoping to catch birds moving out for the afternoon feeding. Again listen for quail, which often whistle in anticipation of going to roost.

Photo by Michael Hanback

Quail often whistle when moving out to feed. Try blowing a quail call morning and afternoon—birds may answer you. Calling is also effective for locating scattered singles after a covey flush.

Late-Season Techniques

Hunting from December through mid-March, depending on location, is preferred by many experienced bobwhite hunters. Here's why.

From middle America north, late-autumn frost or snow has weakened or toppled many grasses and weeds. Across the country, the South included, farm fields have been worked. With cover and food limited, quail concentrate in obvious places, lingering in prime feeding areas morning and evening. This sometimes makes the birds easier for dogs to find and point. However, consider that late-season quail, especially those that have been hunted

Photo by Leonard Lee Rue III

On frigid mornings, bobwhites wait for the winter sun to bathe the countryside before venturing out to feed. Hunt a field edge too early, and you might miss birds.

moderately hard for several months, are typically wild and spooky. Coveys may run and flush wildly out of range; singles may sail half a mile out of sight.

The late-season quail hunter should not hunt too early on the coldest mornings. Bobwhites will wait for the first subtle rays of the winter sun to bathe the fields in pink before venturing out to feed. Go at sunrise and hunt the edges for feeding coveys for an hour or two.

Then return to the nastiest cover you can find during midday. While new-breed bobwhites may loaf in dense brush and deep timber year-round, you can bet they will be huddled there late autumn through winter. With your dogs working closely, hunt prime security covers in zigzag or circling patterns, scouring the cover thoroughly.

Hunting the prime hours prior to sunset is a fine time to catch coveys moving into weed fields and crop edges, including plowed soil, for the afternoon feed. If you find a covey or two, shoot a few birds and leave the singles. Obviously, you should never overshoot coveys, especially late in the year. This will help ensure quail in the area next season.

And try not to break up coveys too late in the afternoon, when they cannot regroup before nightfall. Bobwhites are highly susceptible to cold weather and depend on the warmth of covey circles to survive the coldest nights. Roosting singles are easy prey for night-stalking predators like owls and foxes. Generally a small covey of quail is rarely able to survive the severest winter. Hunt ethically, as you would for any species, to ensure quality quail hunting in the future.

Approach and Gunning Tips

Two key elements will dramatically increase your shooting success on bobwhites, or any quail for that matter.

First, approach a pointing dog strategically. Upon flushing on an edge, a covey of quail will burst quickly, and

Photo by Michael Hanback

When hunting late in the year, shooting a couple of birds from a covey and leaving the singles is the smart, ethical thing to do. This helps ensure healthy quail numbers in the area next season.

fly the shortest route into thick escape cover. If possible, never approach a pointing dog from the side, where you will have only tough, quick-crossing shots on birds angling for cover. Circle the dog until positioned where you can snap shoot quail boring straightaway into thickets or woods. An alternative, though the quick-draw shooting is much more demanding, is to place yourself between a frozen dog and escape cover, where the flushed quail will whip over your head. Remember to take short steps as you approach your dog's point. This provides you with better shooting balance.

Bobwhites over pointing dogs are not difficult to hit if you focus upon one bird. Obviously you should never shoot wildly into a flushing covey. When the covey rises, while shouldering your shotgun concentrate on the first quail that catches your eye. Stay

Photo by Dave Murrian, Tennessee Wildlife Resources Agency

If possible, walk in behind pointing dogs where you'll enjoy straightaway shots at bobwhites beelining for the nearest security cover.

focused upon the bird until you fold it cleanly. Only then should you swing for a double.

Where to Go

Wild bobwhites are hunted in 35 states today. Good to excellent shooting can be found, mostly on private farms, ranches and plantations, in all Southern states, from Florida to Texas. Oklahoma offers some of the finest wild quail hunting in North America. Midwestern and Mid-Atlantic states offer fair to good, if scattered, gunning. Limited opportunities exist in southern New England.

CHAPTER 8

WESTERN QUAIL

There are five huntable species of quail — valley, mountain, scaled, Gambel's and Mearns'— that inhabit the Western United States. They can be divided into two categories:

- **Far West Quail**
- **Desert Quail**

Living in the bobwhite's far-reaching shadow, these quail have received little fanfare over the years. Today, however, the popularity of Western quail hunting is on the rise, for good reason.

Photo by Len Rue, Jr.

The scaled quail and four other Western species have three things in common. All are uniquely handsome, all live in big, challenging country to hunt, and all provide sporty wingshooting.

Regardless of species, western quail are strikingly beautiful. And what a challenge to hunt! They live in big, sprawling, harsh environments, where finding a covey requires considerable walking. Then the hunting really becomes tough. Most western quail are conditioned track stars, running wildly from dogs and hunters, scurrying through prickly deserts or up steep mountainsides. If and when they flush, it is often on the fringe of range, providing sporty wingshooting for the most seasoned bird hunter.

THE FAR WEST QUAIL

The far west quail category includes the valley and mountain species.

Range

Valley or California quail, *Callipepla californica,* are found from Baja north through most of California, Oregon and Washington, into southern British Columbia. They range east into Idaho, Nevada and Utah.

Photo by Len Rue, Jr.   Photo by Bob Robb

The California or valley quail (left) is a striking gamebird, its beauty enhanced by its long, dark "top knot." Standing 12 inches tall and weighing nine ounces, the mountain quail (right) is the largest quail in North America.

Source: **Grouse and Quails of North America,** *Johnsgard*

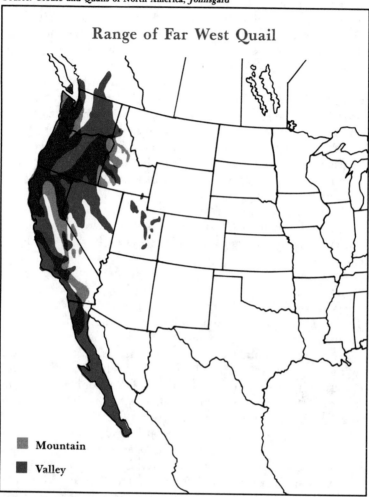

Range of Far West Quail

■ **Mountain**

■ **Valley**

Mountain quail, *Oreortyx pictus,* range from Baja north through California and along the western portions of Oregon and Washington.

Biology and Behavior

Valley quail are beautiful gamebirds. Males are gray with "scaled" coppery breasts. Their brown sides and wings are streaked in white. Their long, slender heads feature scaling patterns on the neck, white facial markings and black throat patches. Long, black plumes or "top knots" curling from the head make the species distinctive. Females are duller in color than males. The quail are about 10 inches long and weigh six ounces.

As its name implies, the valley quail is a bird of valleys and foothills. It prefers low-lying sagebrush, chaparral and other brushlands. The quail feed on seeds, berries, leaves and other flora. They typically water daily in streams, ponds or stock tanks.

Valley quail nest in April, building nests in relatively open areas beneath brush or amid rocks. Females lay and incubate 12 to 15 buff-colored eggs, which hatch in about 22 days.

California quail roost in shrubs or trees. When flushed, the birds prefer to run but will take to the air in small bursts of flight.

Known for their liveliness, valley quail are always on the move, scurrying here and there. In fall, coveys of 40 to 60 birds are common.

Approximately 12 inches long and weighing up to nine ounces, mountain quail are the largest quail in North America. Males are gray overall with chestnut flanks striped in black and white. The birds have brown throat patches, and long, straight plumes jut from their heads. Females are drab with shorter plumes.

As its name implies, the mountain quail is a bird of Western hills and ridges, inhabiting elevations up to 10,000 feet. Habitat consists of dense high-country brush, edges of conifer forests and fringes of clearcuts and alpine meadows. Mountain quail feed upon the leaves, buds and berries of a variety of native plants. They consume pine seeds, acorns and other fruits.

Mountain quail nest in brush. Females may lay 8 to 22 eggs, but commonly 10 to 12, which hatch in about 23 days.

Coveys are small, typically from seven to 20 birds. Mountain quail roost on the ground or in low shrubbery. When disturbed, the birds are swift runners who escape predators by scurrying long distances through impenetrable cover. Back in the densest thickets, they often sit tightly to avoid danger.

Far West Quail Hunting Tactics

Valley Quail Techniques

Private ranches throughout the California quail's range provide excellent habitat for the birds, so obtain permission to bird hunt one of these farms. Large fall coveys will glean leftover grain in

Photo by Bob Robb

Field edges in oak foothills are fine places to flush valley quail.

agricultural fields, and pick up spilled livestock feed in pastures. The birds can also be found feeding on weed seeds in brushy ravines, stream bottoms and grasslands rimming ranches.

Scout after sunrise through midmorning, riding or walking ranch roads, searching for coveys of gray, plumed birds scattered across open feeding areas. Binoculars can be a great help. Look carefully in and around the fringes of fields. Dense escape cover, such as brushy thickets, sapling jungles or low conifers, will likely be within short flying or running distance.

Upon locating a feeding covey, keep your dogs in close and approach carefully. You might not get shooting at birds in the open. Chances are, several dozen sharp eyes will spot you, and the quail will run into thick escape cover.

That is all right, for in that dense cover valley birds, like most quail, sit tight, often seemingly impossible to flush. For this reason many valley quail hunters prefer Labs or other flushing dogs for rooting birds from security cover.

Noon through mid-afternoon, look for California quail on the shady edges of security cover, or near a water source. Hunt feeding areas again in late afternoon. Listen for the "key-car-go" calling of birds anytime of day, but particularly in evening as feeding birds begin assembling for roosting. Zero into this calling and you can often slip strategically into range of a covey.

Like bobwhites, coveys of California quail have small home territories that they inhabit year after year. They will often walk

Photo by Bob Robb

Binoculars can help you locate western quail, especially early in the morning when coveys are scattered, active and feeding. Glass hillsides and fields for moving birds, and look for a sentinel quail perched atop brushy cover.

Photo by Bob Robb

Many valley quail hunters prefer springer spaniels and Labs for routing tight-sitting singles from thick cover.

long distances to prime feeding areas day after day. Use these routines to your advantage by patterning the birds season after season. Concentrate your daily hunting in prime feeding, resting and roosting areas.

Mountain Quail Techniques

Mountain quail hunting is unique. The high-country habitat reminds one of spruce and blue grouse country. Yet the behavior of the running, unpredictable, often wildly flushing quail is akin to the habits of eastern ruffed grouse. These quail are truly a challenge. They are underhunted in many areas.

Like valley quail, mountain birds have small home ranges, often nestled in secluded, remote hills and ridges. Combined with the fact that mountain quail are found in small coveys, this makes the birds difficult to find.

Search brush-laced mountain habitats, such as stream bottoms and the edges of clearcuts and meadows. If possible hunt these areas as you would the lairs of any mountain game — from above or on the same plane. If you hunt from below, the birds will simply run uphill and disappear into escape cover before you are anywhere near shooting range.

One good tactic is to put your dogs, or a hunting partner, into a creek bottom, draw or other prime cover while you walk parallel along a high ridge. You might even try blocking the upper end of a valley or canyon. This allows you to cut off birds running uphill. If you surprise them, you can get reasonably good shooting. A bird or two might even wing back over the cover, offering shots for your partner.

Photo by Bob Robb

Hunting moderately steep, open hillsides laced with shrubs and understory will often yield a mountain quail or two.

In fall, mountain quail move down from their alpine summer range to inhabit moderately steep, but relatively open, hillsides.

Photo by Bob Robb

Putting a partner and dogs in a draw while you walk parallel along a high ridgeline is an effective way of cutting off quail that sprint up a mountainside.

Photo by Bob Robb

California is your best bet for shooting a limit of both valley and mountain quail.

Prime spots to hunt are south-facing hillsides with a diversified mixture of low trees, understory and grass. Hunt midmorning for birds feeding upon leaves, seeds and buds. Check nearby security cover during afternoon.

Where to Go

California offers the best hunting for both valley and mountain quail. For valley birds, good opportunities also exist in Washington, Oregon, Idaho, Nevada and British Columbia. Oregon, Washington and Nevada offer fair to good hunting for mountain quail.

The Desert Quail

The desert quail category encompasses the scaled, Gambel's and Mearns' birds.

Range

Scaled quail, *Callipepla squamata*, often called "blues" or "cotton-tops" by Westerners, can be found throughout western Texas, west through New Mexico, into eastern Arizona. The birds range north through the Oklahoma panhandle, into Colorado.

The Gambel's quail, *Callipepla gambelii*, ranges from southwest Texas west through southern and central New Mexico, across the southern tier of Arizona, into southern Nevada and California.

The Mearns', *Cyrtonyx montezumae*, also known as the harlequin or Montezuma quail, is concentrated in southern New Mexico and southern Arizona.

Biology and Behavior

The scaled quail is 10 to 12 inches long and weighs about six ounces. Sexes are similar in appearance. Birds are grayish-brown with distinctive, dark-edged, scaled breast and neck feathers. Instead of a plume, scaled quail have white-tipped crests upon their heads.

Scaled quail inhabit desert plateaus covered with sage, mesquite, creosote and cacti. The birds are also found in grasslands, preferring brushy washes, canyons and river bottoms. In these wild environments, scaled quail feed upon the seeds of weeds and shrubs.

Source: Grouse and Quails of North America, *Johnsgard*

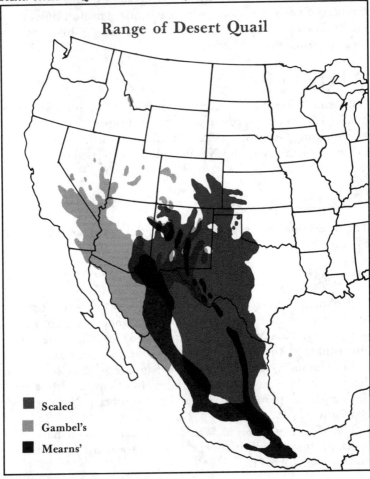

Range of Desert Quail

Scaled

Gambel's

Mearns'

The birds will flock to the edges of southwestern ranches when possible. Here they glean grain and water daily at stock tanks.

Scaled quail nest in shallow depressions beneath brush or grass. Each spring with sufficient desert rainfall, females lay 10 to 15 eggs and incubate them in 22 days.

Scaled quail are often found in huge coveys, up to 100 birds. These quail are legendary runners, preferring to sprint rather than fly at the first sign of predators, dogs or hunters.

The Gambel's quail is about 10 inches long and weighs six

Photo by Leonard Lee Rue III

Scaled or blue quail inhabit either deserts or grasslands.

ounces. Males are the customary gray "desert camouflage," with brown, white-streaked sides and chestnut throat patches. They have white facial stripes and black patches on lower breasts. Sprouting from their burnt-orange-crowned heads are short, curved black plumes. Females are duller in color.

Gambel's quail inhabit mesquite thickets, chaparral-covered ravines and covers of thorny trees, shrubs and cacti. Here they feed on seeds, fruits and leaves.

Female Gambel's construct haphazard nests in shallow depressions. They lay nine to 15 eggs and incubate them in 23 days.

Gambel's roost in shrubs and stunted desert trees. In fall they

Photo by Bob Miles, Arizona Game and Fish Department

Like most Western quail, the Gambel's is a runner. At the first hint of danger, quail scurry across the desert floor.

Photo by Judd Cooney

With its distinctive, white-marked face, the Mearns' is the oddest looking quail in North America.

typically gather in coveys of 10 to 15 birds. But running across a bevy of 50 birds is not uncommon. Gambel's prefer sprinting to flying when disturbed.

Mearns' quail are eight inches long and weigh six ounces. Males are mottled gray and brown and flecked with white and black. Their uniquely patterned heads and faces make the Mearns' the oddest looking of North American quail. Their faces are bluish-black with distinctive white swirls. Brown crests extend down their necks. Female Mearns' are duller with less prominent facial markings.

Photo by Judd Cooney

Unlike other desert quail, which typically gather in large coveys, Mearns' travel in pairs or small family groups.

126

Mearns' are birds of the high desert, inhabiting grassy canyons, rocky ravines and woodlands up to 9,000 feet. Distinctively long toes and claws allow them to negotiate rugged terrain and dig for favorite foods like chufa bulbs. The birds also scratch up seeds and acorns.

Females construct elaborate nests between April and September. They lay 10 to 12 white eggs, incubated by both sexes in 25 days.

Unlike other desert quail, Mearns' travel in pairs or small family groups. When pressured, they often sit tightly or flush with swift bursts of speed.

Desert Quail Hunting Tactics

Photo by Bob Robb

Living side by side in many parts of their southwestern range (though blue quail inhabit grasslands to the north and east) scaled and Gambel's quail have similar habits. Therefore, hunting techniques in the prime desert covers are similar.

Both scaled and Gambel's follow the daily routine of all quail: They eat early, then loaf during midday. After

Low-lying desert washes are fine places for a hunter and flushing dog to find plenty of desert quail.

feeding, instead of heading for the thickest available security cover, desert birds are often found loitering around water. In good desert quail habitat, the countryside surrounding any water source is a fine place to bird hunt.

A good tactic is to walk or ride backcountry roads, searching for birds loafing around a stream bed, pond or stock tank. Binoculars can help you zero in on coveys of watering quail.

If you spot no birds, approach the water source itself, looking for quail tracks, droppings and dusting areas. If large coveys are using the area, sign will be abundant. Interestingly, since desert

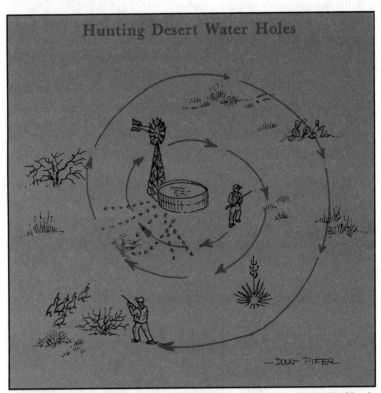

Hunting Desert Water Holes

—DOUG PIFER

In the desert, water is a magnet for scaled and Gambel's quail. Check around ponds, stock tanks and streams for tracks, droppings and dusting bowls. Then hunt in ever-widening circles until you run across birds moving into or away from the water source.

quail are walking birds, you can often track them to and from water.

Anytime of day, hunt around the water hole. Zigzag the cover or sweep out from the water in ever-widening circles. This allows you to locate quail moving to and from water.

Having located a covey of birds, approach slowly at first. If you pressure desert quail from afar, they will run great distances. This can make them difficult or impossible to locate a second time.

If fortunate enough to get the drop on a covey, then pressure the birds, running, yelling, flailing your arms, doing what you must to make them fly. Flushing dogs trained to work close, scent trail running birds and put them into the air are excellent.

When a covey erupts, remember to concentrate on one bird while shooting. Then swing for a double while trying to mark the singles. This is often tough to do in big, sprawling country that looks alike, but try this tip. Watch where the majority of quail sail down, then look up on the horizon and select a butte, cactus or other prominent landmark. Walk a straight line toward the marker until you find singles. While desert quail are notorious runners, they often sit tightly after a covey rise. This works to your advantage using the above technique.

Finally, listen for calling quail to pinpoint their location. Scaled quail often whistle "pe-cos", Gambel's "chi-ca-go-go" early in the morning or in late afternoon.

Rising from the harsh, arid deserts of Arizona and New Mexico can be found microcosms of great mountain ranges, the "high desert." On these hills and ridges, some high enough to accumulate snow in winter months, and in valleys and canyons laced

Photo by Bob Robb

When a covey of quail levels out across the sprawling desert, it's hard to mark singles while shooting. Watch where the birds settle down, then look straight up on the horizon for a prominent landmark. Walk a direct line toward your marker until you flush singles.

129

with rocks, cacti, yucca, grasses and scrub oak you'll find the intriguing Mearns' quail.

Remember, Mearns' have long toes and claws. These they use to scratch below scrub oak for acorns, bulbs and tubers. Finding this sign is one of the best ways to locate Mearns' quail. The hunting is akin to searching for wild turkeys in the fall, though Mearns' quail do not venture nearly as far as scratching wild turkeys.

Walk high-desert hills and ridges, looking for scratchings on the edges of grasslands, from early morning to late afternoon. Hunt from the same plane or above where you anticipate birds if possible. Use a pointing dog if practical for you. Unlike other desert quail, the Mearns' will hold nicely for a gundog. In this regard the species has been compared to the bobwhite. But

Photo by Bob Miles, Arizona Game and Fish Department

Walk high-desert hills and ridges laced with scrub oak, hoping to find Mearns' quail scratching up acorns. Use a pointing dog if you like — the Mearns' is the one western quail that sits nicely for a gundog.

Mearns' fly faster, and more unpredictably, when flushed. Then the singles really sit tight. You and your dog will have to scour the country, often several times over, or you will step right over the singles.

Where to Go

Top states for scaled quail include New Mexico, Arizona and Colorado. Good opportunities also exist in Texas, Oklahoma and Kansas. For Gambel's Arizona is tops, followed by California and New Mexico. Mearns' quail hunting is best in Arizona.

CHAPTER 9

PHEASANTS

Photo by Michael Hanback

The ring-necked pheasant, imported from Asia in the late 1800s, has become a favorite of upland gunners, particularly in midwestern and the western grassland states where pheasant populations are highest.

 As if shot from a spring-loaded trap, a cock pheasant leaps high into the crisp autumn sky. Hanging amid the brilliant blue, against amber waves of grain that shimmer lightly to the horizon, the bird is a rainbow of colors, flashing iridescently green, blue, purple and bronze in the intense afternoon sunshine. Its white-ringed neck shines brightly, its long, black-barred tail grazes the tips of grassy cover as the rooster cackles nosily away.

Such a vision is undoubtedly one of the most spectacular in bird hunting. There is simply no other species in the upland kingdom that rivals the ring-necked pheasant's vivid beauty. Yet the rooster pheasant has other attributes as well. A runner with excellent eyesight, hearing and survival instincts, the pheasant is challenging to locate and pin for both hunter and dog. A tough, strong flier, the ringneck is a formidable target, especially on windy days and late in the season. There is perhaps no other bird more celebrated and delicious on the table. Little wonder this Asian immigrant is one of the most popular upland gamebirds in North America today.

Like bobwhite quail hunting, the pursuit of wild ringnecks is a different ball game today than it was decades ago. Pheasant populations vary widely from area to area, fluctuating season to season. Changing habitat — shrinking in some areas, still expansive clean farming with heavy use of chemicals in others — has forced the birds to modify their behavior while adapting to new covers.

To be successful the modern hunter should modify his technique as well. After first examining the ringneck's range, biology and behavior, this chapter focuses upon several time-tested tactics, laced with new twists, that should produce fine gunning all season long in today's ever-changing pheasant covers.

Range

The earliest recorded attempt to introduce pheasants into North America occurred in 1733, when the governor of New York imported a dozen pairs of English black-necked pheasants. All pheasants are of Asia and Asia Minor ancestries, though the birds had been established in Europe for centuries prior to introductions attempted in North America.

The first significant importation of pheasants occurred 110 years ago when Judge Owen Denny, then consul general to Shanghai, shipped 50 to 70 birds from the Orient to his homestead

Source: Pheasants Forever, Inc.

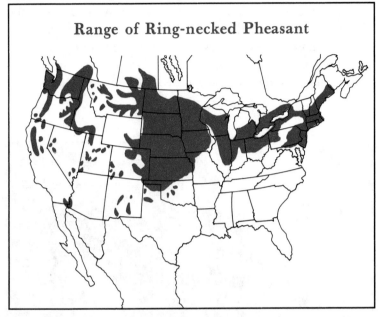

Range of Ring-necked Pheasant

in the Wilamette Valley in Oregon. Within 10 years (1892) the birds had so populated that area of Oregon that the first pheasant hunting season was held; 50,000 birds were harvested on that opening day and the season continued for 75 days.

There are two species of true pheasants with 34 subspecies. Our common ringneck, *Phasianus colchicus*, is a mixture of many different sub-species imported from Asian and European stock.

Over the past century, this gamebird has greatly expanded its range, thanks to the bird's adaptability and successful stocking programs. Today, ringnecks are found from coast to coast across the northern United States. Pheasants range as far north as south-central British Columbia, Alberta and Saskatchewan; as far south as Texas, New Mexico and Southern California.

Biology and Behavior

A rooster pheasant is a large gamebird, 30 to 35 inches long, 20 inches of which may be its black-barred tail. Average weight is 2½ to 3 pounds. The cock pheasant is a menagerie of splendid colors. Its body is coppery brown with black, brown and white

135

flecking; its breast radiates a purplish-green sheen. The male has an iridescent purple, green and blue head with red facial wattles. The cock bird's distinctive white neck ring gives the species its name. A rooster has leg spurs, which it uses to challenge other males during spring breeding season. A hen pheasant, smaller and lacking spurs, is mottled brown with a shorter tail.

Photo by Bob Lollo

A mature rooster has a prominent white neck ring. Its black-barred tail may be 20 inches long.

Wild ring-necked pheasants are primarily farmland birds, inhabiting corn, barley, milo and wheat country, feeding upon spilled grain. The birds also feed on insects and weed seeds and pick up and consume some grit to grind food. Thick, brushy hedgerows, fence lines, shelterbelts, ditches, woodlots, sloughs and marshes rimming croplands provide resting and roosting cover for the birds. Pheasants can be found in good numbers in midwestern and western grasslands and short-grass prairies.

Pheasants live their entire lives within two square miles of land, where their living requirements for cover and food must be met. In addition, travel ways between habitat types must exist.

Ring-necked pheasants flourished throughout their range during the 1940s and 50s when land-use practices were ideal.

Photos by Leonard Lee Rue III

A hen pheasant is drab-brown and smaller than a rooster. Hens nest in brushy fields or ditches, laying seven to 12 eggs. Chicks hatch in 23–25 days.

Abundance reached as high as 400 birds per square mile of land in many parts of the country.

Pheasants are polygamous, meaning a rooster will breed a number of hens each spring. One male commonly breeds with 10 to 12 females. As a wild turkey struts and gobbles, a wild rooster pheasant struts and crows to attract hens to his home turf, which may cover a mile or two. Receptive females move into a rooster's territory, and after copulation build nests in grassy fields or in brushy ditches or sloughs. Hens lay 8 to 15 greenish-brown eggs, incubating them in 23 days.

Pheasants are persistent renesters; if a nest is destroyed hens have been known to attempt as many as four renestings. But each time a hen is forced to renest, the clutch decreases. For example, if the first attempt contained 9 eggs the third might have only four. Thus, productivity decreases.

Ringnecks are often gregarious in late autumn and winter, gathering in flocks of 30 to 40 birds. At times, flocks of 100 pheasants may be spotted in prime winter feeding and roosting areas. Roosters often flock with fellow roosters, hens with hens.

Like all upland gamebirds, pheasants possess excellent eyesight and hearing. When danger approaches, the birds are notorious runners, scurrying through grasslands, croplands and thick brush with tails cocked upward. When pressured into flushing, roosters often rocket straight up into the sky, rising in whirs of wings and cackling noisily. But the birds can sail away quietly as well. Having flushed from cover and composed himself in the air, a rooster can fly up to 40 mph.

Pheasant Hunting Tactics

Distinguishing Roosters

Wild pheasant hunting is unique in that only cock birds are legal targets in the majority of areas. To hunt legally and ethically, you must be able to distinguish roosters from hens.

At first glance this may seem simple. Who could mistake a short-tailed, drab-brown hen for a gaudy, long-tailed cock bird? But it can easily happen in the heat of gunning, especially if a bird flushes at long range, from dense cover or directly into the sun.

If a pheasant flushes and you have your doubts, look for the tell-tale white neck ring, present only on roosters. If you cannot see this ring, pass up the shot. Zeroing in on this white collar has an added advantage: Tracking the neck ring while pulling the trigger keeps you swinging your shotgun out front of a flushing rooster, which, with its long tail, can be a deceptive flier easily shot behind.

Early-Season Techniques

In top pheasant hunting states across the country, as many as

Photo by Leonard Lee Rue

Look for a cock bird's white neck ring and long tail before firing. Tracking the neck ring keeps your shotgun swinging on the front end of a hard-flying rooster.

half of the ringnecks harvested each year may be shot during the first week of the season. Why? This is when most hunters are afield. And these hunters are shooting a lot of uneducated young-of-the-year roosters.

Early in the season, both young and mature roosters are often found in relatively hospitable cover to hunt, such as short-grass hayfields and prairies, thin-brush ditches and hedgerows, and standing crops. Roosters often run wildly in tall corn and flush out of sight.

With food plentiful and pheasants ranging across sprawling cover, this is the time for classic pheasant drives all day long. Here's how to use the time-tested technique to full advantage today.

First, choose a field that your party can cover thoroughly. Depending on field size, effective driving can require from 5 to 20 or more guns.

Several standers or blockers sneak quietly into place at one end of the field, preferably the edge with the least available cover. Post enough hunters to cover all corners and other obvious escape routes. If possible, blockers should set up with the sun behind them. This will make flushing roosters easy to see and shoot.

Photo by James M. Norine

In early autumn, a hunting party driving fields, sloughs and ditches can expect excellent results. In many areas, half of the roosters harvested each year are shot during the first week of the season.

The remaining drivers, with or without dogs, begin at the opposite end of the field, preferably laced with the thickest cover. Pushing birds from dense to thin cover should lead to more flushes.

The drivers should line up parallel, spaced far enough apart to scour the field, yet close enough to keep ringnecks from running back between the line. The drivers then move slowly and quietly forward.

A pair of flankers on each end of the line walks 30 yards or so ahead of the drivers. This keeps roosters from escaping out the sides of the field.

While early in the season drivers and flankers may enjoy some shooting at young roosters that flush before the moving line of guns, the purpose of driving is to force ringnecks, which see, hear and sense the drivers, to run to the edge of the field — straight into the blockers. Then, feeling nervous and trapped, the roosters flush before the waiting guns. Some birds may then whip back over the line of hunters, offering challenging, overhead shooting.

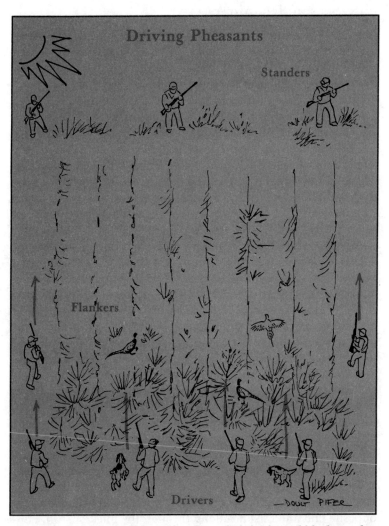

Driving Pheasants

Standers

Flankers

Drivers

—DOUG PIFER

If possible, hunters should put the sun to their backs and block an edge with thin cover. Drivers and dogs enter the thick side of a field and move slowly forward. A pair of flankers helps keep roosters from running out the sides.

Driving pheasants with a party of hunters obviously requires the utmost in firearms safety. Shotguns must be handled and pointed safely. Both the blockers and drivers must keep track of each other at all times. Only high-flying roosters that flush into safe zones should be shot.

Late-Season Techniques

Late in the year, many young pheasants have been shot by driving hunters. Those birds that survive, having passed a crash course in survival, become highly educated. The mature roosters, the wiliest of all, become really tough. So why hunt late?

First, with fewer hunters afield there is less competition. And since most croplands have been harvested or worked, pheasants are concentrated in obvious pockets.

This will likely be the densest, nastiest cover available. Prime late-season pheasant haunts involve brushy ditches, woodland edges, cattail sloughs, anyplace a rooster can burrow out of the cold and wind and out of sight of predators. If there is grain stubble nearby, so much the better. Pheasants will venture out to feed early and late in the day.

As mentioned, fewer hunters venture out late in the season. This is likely a time when you must hunt alone or with a dedicated partner or two. While a good pheasant dog is a great help anytime of season, it is often a prerequisite to success late in the year. A well-trained pointing or flushing breed will add excitement and enjoyment to the hunt. A good hunting dog can also scent trail and pin or flush hard-running roosters. A dog is valuable for running down and retrieving tough-to-kill pheasants.

As you would in any type of late-season bird hunting, concentrate your pheasant strategy on the sunlit, south-facing edges of cover each morning, especially if it is brutally cold. Roosters thrive on warming themselves in the subtle winter sun. Vary your hunting throughout the day to follow the direction of the sun; scour areas where warm rays continuously slice into the cover.

If hunting with a partner, an effective way to hunt late-season cover is to pull a midday mini-drive. While your partner blocks one edge of a cover, you, preferably with a dog, return to the opposite end and bust headlong through the thickest stuff, hoping to run a rooster or two his way. The key to success is to select the right cover to hunt. A narrow thicket, woodlot, slough or marsh bordered by open fields is prime. If you choose too big a cover strip, roosters will evade you by circling.

When hunting alone without the services of a dog, choosing manageable cover is even more critical. Hunt the narrowest draws, ditches or sloughs you can find. Work from thickest to thinnest cover, with eyes peeled for a running rooster. If you spot grass whipping before you, circle ahead and, using caution, run at the pheasant, hopefully pressuring a rooster into flight.

Photo by Maslowski

Photo by Bob Lollo

Late in the season, hunt for pheasants in brushy ditches, cattail sloughs woodland edges and corn stubbles, where roosters seek shelter from cold winds, snow and predators.

If forced to hunt a sizable field or block of prairie, either with a partner or solo, try this technique. Beginning near the center of the field, hunt slowly, zigzagging toward one corner. Try to force roosters into the V of the corner; pressure any running ringnecks right to the edge. This is the only effective way to make them fly. Return to the middle of the field and push the remaining three corners in search of roosters.

Ringnecks are notorious runners, but they are uncannily unpredictable. Sometimes roosters will sit tightly late in the season,

143

Photo by Leonard Lee Rue III

A springer spaniel can be excellent for scent trailing and flushing running pheasants. After the shot, the dog is invaluable for retrieving tough roosters.

Photo by Michael Hanback

A pair of hunters "mini-driving" a narrow ditch or slough is an excellent way to bag a rooster or two.

hiding in thick cover of course, but often lying behind a clump of dirt, tuft of grass or other small, often overlooked tidbit of cover. When hunting alone or with a partner, hunt a few yards, then stop for 30 seconds or so before moving 10 yards farther ahead. This stop-and-go technique can be unnerving to a hiding rooster who, having lost track of the intruding predator, may explode into the air to escape potential danger.

Finally, in most parts of the pheasant's range snow blankets the earth late in the season. After a storm, freshly fallen snow allows tracking opportunities. Following pheasant tracks (if prints are mingled together, the slightly larger ones should be a rooster's) may not lead directly to shooting roosters; spooky upon the white canvas of snow, cockbirds will likely run and flush wildly. But tracking tells you birds are in the area, which covers they are using, and from which direction they are entering the thickets. This allows you to concentrate your hunting and put dogs and/or blockers and drivers strategically into hot covers.

Special Choke/Load Considerations

As compared to other types of upland bird hunting, where one shotgun choke/load combination is normally sufficient all season, pheasant hunting is unique. It is common for ringneck hunters to tailor gauges, chokes and loads to early and late seasons.

Early, when roosters typically flush within 25 yards, either a 12- or 20-gauge choked improved cylinder (and modified with a double gun) shooting high-power 7½s is a fine choice.

Late, when roosters are often running and flushing at long range, some hunters rely on a 12-gauge exclusively and screw in modified or even full choke tubes. They sometimes upgrade to 2¾- or even 3-inch magnum 4s and 6s. This can be effective if you hunt hard-pressured birds without a dog in big country, but you might find yourself overgunned if you use a close-working shorthair, springer or Lab and concentrate on the thickest winter cover available. Here, when routing out roosters that normally flush 15 to 40 yards, you would probably be best served with a 12-gauge shooting high-power 6s or 7½s, or a 20-gauge shooting 3-inch magnum 6s.

Photo by Leonard Lee Rue III

Early in the season, either a 20- or 12-gauge choked improved cylinder or modified, shooting high-power No. 6s or 7½s, is a fine choice for close-rising pheasants. Later, when roosters often flush at long range, you may need to use a 12 exclusively, screw in a modified or full choke tube and upgrade to magnum 4s, 5s or 6s.

Where to Go

The Midwest and the western grasslands are classic pheasant country. The ringneck is the state bird of South Dakota, where fine pheasant hunting is found. Iowa, Nebraska, Kansas, Michigan, Minnesota, Wisconsin and North Dakota offer good to excellent hunting most years.

Out west, Montana, Idaho, Oregon, Washington and California are top states. In the Northeast, Pennsylvania shows a better-than-average annual pheasant harvest. Scattered pockets in other northern and central states offer hunting opportunities. With the exception of north central Maryland, wild pheasants do not reproduce well south of the Mason-Dixon Line. Except for certain pockets, ringneck hunting in the Southeast is restricted to preserve birds.

CHAPTER 10
RUFFED GROUSE

Hunt ruffed grouse anywhere they occur in North America, and you're in for a challenging day afield. Whether in Northern aspens or Appalachian Mountain hardwoods, the birds will be found inhabiting thick, rugged, inhospitable covers. In these situations, grouse are unpredictable. They can thunder up seemingly beneath your boot soles or flush silently 50 yards in front of your gundog. Once airborne, ruffed grouse may dodge behind saplings before you can pull the trigger, fishhook down at 100 yards or sail over a ridge and out of the country. Who knows? But one thing is certain: Each autumn or winter day that you walk in glorious grouse country, experiencing the unnerving explosion of wings, glimpsing silvery or

Photo by Maslowski

One of the most strikingly beautiful gamebirds in North America, the ruffed grouse is also unpredictable and a challenge to hunt.

coppery feathers boring through keyholes in timber, you'll marvel at this intriguing upland gamebird. As the sun sets on each long, tough day of hunting, you'll leave a cover tired but happy, whether you've shot a grouse or two or drawn a blank.

Range

No less than 12 subspecies of ruffed grouse, *Bonasa umbellus*, inhabit North America. A prominent bird of the North Country, the grouse is found coast to coast throughout Canada, ranging into central Alaska.

In the eastern United States, ruffed grouse range from Maine south to northern Georgia, inhabiting the Appalachian Mountain corridor. In the mid-United States the birds range south through Michigan, Wisconsin and Minnesota. In the West, grouse range south through Idaho, into northern Utah, and into western portions of Washington and Oregon. Isolated populations are found in Iowa, Illinois, Indiana and Missouri. Experimental transplanting programs are underway in several states in efforts to expand the ruffed grouse's range.

Source: **Grouse and Quails of North America,** *Johnsgard*

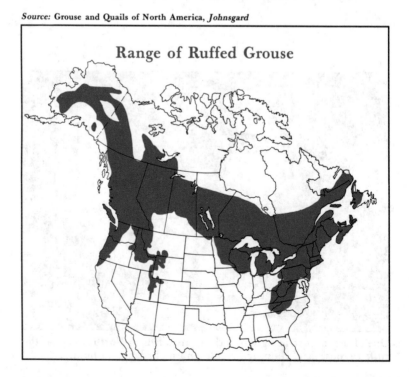

Range of Ruffed Grouse

Biology and Behavior

Ruffed grouse, also regionally known as partridge or mountain pheasant, are medium-sized gamebirds, 15 to 19 inches long and weighing around 1½ pounds. Mature males are larger than hens.

Ruffed grouse are found in two color phases: gray and brown/red. Authorities speculate that color phases may be tied closely to habitat and exist to provide heat absorption or dissipation and natural camouflage. Such camouflage helps grouse elude predators. Gray-phase birds are typically found in the dense conifer forests of Canada and Alaska, the aspen and birch coverts of the northern United States and the mountainous west. Brown and reddish grouse inhabit eastern and southeastern oak woodlands, and coastal regions in Oregon and Washington.

At a glance in the field, male and female ruffed grouse appear identical. Depending on the birds' gray, brown or reddish coloration, breast feathers, lying in a barred pattern, are light gray, buff or white. The birds' backs are flecked with gray, buff or white.

Both cocks and hens wear beautiful neck ruffs, hence the name ruffed grouse. These neck feathers are typically brown or black, but red in some instances. Neck ruffs are most noticeable on adult males. When fully erected, these long, iridescent feathers encircle the upper neck in a spectacular display. All grouse have erectile crests upon their heads.

The ruffed grouse's glory, its distinctive tail, is comprised of 16 to 18 long, thin feathers called rectrices. Grouse fan their tails when strutting and in flight. Interestingly, these rectrices act like rudders, controlling a grouse's direction in flight.

A coppery-red, brown or black subterminal band rims a grouse's tail. For years, hunters have assumed that a "broken" band—the two center feathers either shorter or their banding lighter in color or fuzzier than the rest of the tail—indicates a hen grouse. This is often the case, but many cock grouse have broken bands as well.

A more reliable sex indicator is tail length. Place a mature male and female grouse side and side, and the cock bird will have longer tail feathers. Some biologists say that a grouse with tail feathers over six inches long is probably a male. Many authorities point out that a hen's tail is normally as long as its back, while a mature cock's tail is noticeably longer than its back.

Another method to determine the sex of ruffed grouse is to examine the details of certain rump feathers. Pluck two feathers

Photos by Michael Hanback

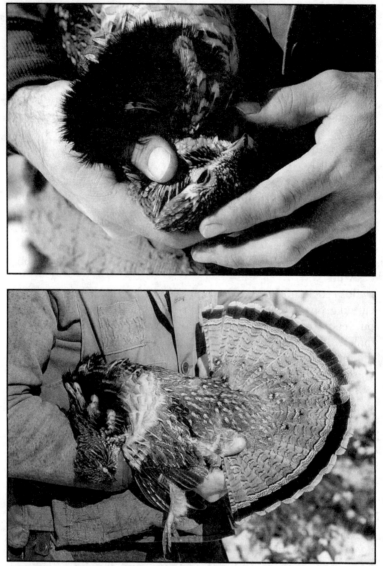

In hand, a mature ruffed grouse's neck ruff and fanned tail are its crowning glories.

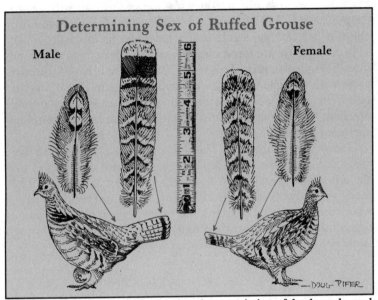

The above illustration details the characteristics of both male and female grouse.

Photo by Len Rue, Jr.

Ruffed grouse feed upon hundreds of species of forest plants. Birds often hop into trees and browse buds in late autumn and winter.

from the lower back of a grouse just above the long stiff coverts. Count the number of white or whitish dots. Females have only one dot per feather, while males have two or more.

Ruffed grouse are forest birds, inhabiting deciduous woodlands interspersed with mixed conifers. Yet they are birds of the edge, preferring overgrown fringes of clearcuts, burns, meadows and old orchards. Second-growth saplings with understory provide excellent habitat, as do cover-rich creek and stream bottoms and sheltered swamps.

Grouse are omnivorous. The chicks are dependent upon a large variety of insect life for added protein. Studies have revealed that the adult birds feast upon hundreds of varieties of flora. They feed primarily on leaves, buds, seeds, fruits, nuts and berries of woodland plants and trees in their range. Like most gallinaceous gamebirds, grouse meet their daily water requirements through the dew-laced, succulent foods they digest.

Photo by Leonard Lee Rue III

The ruffed grouse's drumming is one of nature's most distinctive sounds. In spring, a male steps onto a preferred log and beats his wings rapidly to attract hens to his territory.

Male ruffed grouse drum in springtime, stepping onto a favorite log and beating their wings rapidly to attract hens to their territory. When a receptive hen approaches a cock bird's drumming log, the male fans his tail, lifts his ruff and struts in an impressive courtship display.

Females hollow out a nest in leaves, often at the base of a stump, tree, deadfall or rock. From April to July, depending on region, hens lay 9 to 12 cream-colored eggs, which hatch in 24 days. If a hen's nest is disturbed, she will attempt a second brood.

Photos by Leonard Lee Rue III

In springtime, female grouse hollow out a nest in leaves and lay nine to 12 eggs. Chicks hatch in about 24 days.

While grouse typically fly up to roost in saplings and evergreen trees, they also roost on the ground, amid the security of logs, stumps, thick brush or deadfalls. In winter, particularly in northern areas where snow piles up to a foot or more, ruffs may burrow or plunge into "snow roosts," which provide the birds with warming insulation and protection from predators.

Ruffed grouse are scattered and solitary most of the year. In early autumn, young grouse leave the hens, dispersing widely into covers they will call home the rest of their lives. In winter, grouse, old and young alike, often gather loosely in prime feeding and cover areas.

In remote western and northern areas, ruffed grouse, particularly birds of the year, are "fool hens" that sit tightly in plain view of approaching hunters. But in most parts of their range, the birds are educated, wily and wonderfully unpredictable. They thunder up underfoot or flush wildly in an unnerving roar of wings. Grouse may also flush silently, especially when leaving trees. They fly low, rocking and weaving through trees. Ruffed grouse have been clocked at 40 mph.

No discussion of ruffed grouse biology is complete without mention of population dynamics. Woodland birds inhabiting millions of acres of public forest, ruffed grouse have not been as negatively impacted by modern land-use practices as have farm-inhabiting upland birds. On the contrary, such practices as clearcutting, timbering and strip mining have improved ruffed grouse habitat in many areas.

But then there is the celebrated "10-year cycle." While biologists do not fully understand this phenomena — during which grouse populations fluctuate widely from year to year — most agree it does exist, particularly in northern areas. Ongoing studies are examining weather, predation, disease and other mortality factors, as well as changes in grouse movements and reproduction. While theories are inconclusive, the reality remains that from year to year it is often boom or bust in ruffed grouse country.

Ruffed Grouse Hunting Tactics

Finding Grouse Lifelines

The ruffed grouse is the widest ranging, nonmigratory upland gamebird in North America. Throughout the species' sprawling range is a common habitat theme — grouse use diverse forests,

Photo by Joe Workosky

Due to the ruffed grouse's celebrated population cycle, hunting is often boom or bust year to year.

mature woodlands interspersed with stands of second-growth saplings, evergreens and various edge covers. But preferred grouse habitats may vary region to region. To hunt successfully in your area, you must zero in on specific local covers that provide lifelines for ruffed grouse autumn through winter.

In the North and West, find aspen and you will likely find grouse. The birds thrive on aspen buds. Where available, birch and maple are also preferred. To narrow down prime aspen/birch covers to hunt, look for nearby alder thickets and mixed conifers, which provide security and roosting cover for grouse.

In the Midwest, old, overgrown "dirty" fields are preferred feeding areas for grouse. Nearby cedars are security covers to hunt.

If hunting in the Appalachian Mountains of the eastern United States, follow these general guidelines.

In the Northeast, hunt covers laced with food-rich aspen, birch, cherry and hop hornbeam. Nearby conifers will make a cover complete.

In the Mid-Atlantic and Southeast, locate stream bottoms, sidehills and clearcuts laced with mountain laurel and you have

Photo by Charlie Farmer

Photo by Michael Hanback

Discover the ruffed grouse's lifeline in your area, and you'll find birds. Whether hunting the edge of a Rocky Mountain aspen stand or amid a sea of mountain laurel in the Appalachians, grouse will provide endless hours of challenging hunting.

found the lifeline of ruffed grouse. Mountain laurel provides excellent cover. The birds feed voraciously on its leaves and buds in winter. Abandoned farm fields, stands of second-growth oak and greenbriar thickets also provide a variety of foods. Though winters in this region are typically mild, corridors of white pines provide security cover during cold and stormy spells.

Early-Season Techniques

Regardless of where and which type of cover you hunt, ruffed grouse, solitary by nature, will be scattered from October through early November. Food is widely abundant, and the weather is not yet harsh enough to force birds into concentrated pockets of late-autumn and winter cover.

Therefore, you must cover as much country as possible. A pointing dog and a partner or two are a big help, greatly expanding your hunting range each day. Using a pointing dog this time of year has an added advantage: Birds of the year, recently dispersed into unfamiliar covers, often sit nicely for a dog in thick cover, though it can be hot and dry, making scenting conditions tough.

Early in the season, it is difficult to pattern grouse. While they undoubtedly feed morning and afternoon, they often spend the entire day loafing in brushy edges, gleaning a variety of herbs, leaves, seeds and plants. Instead of worrying about hunting a particular feeding or resting area, choose a prime cover and hunt it thoroughly. This gives you the best chance of running across a grouse or two.

Excellent edges to hunt include clearcut fringes, edges of abandoned farm fields and orchards, and borders where second-growth saplings meet mature forest. And never pass up a cover-rich stream bottom; while grouse do not flock there to drink, they rest beneath the typically thick cover, out of sight of predators. Similarly, hunt a spring or other open waterhole in early fall, as there is generally a grouse or two loafing nearby.

Grouse also like to venture out along logging roads that traverse clearcuts. Here they gather grit to mix with their food. A good tactic is walking these lanes in the late afternoon and evening hours.

Hunting on autumn days, you may hear male grouse drumming. Fall drumming should not be confused with the spring mating ritual, rather it is a physical response to declining daylight hours. Some biologists say grouse drum outside the breeding

Photo by John Hall, Vermont Department of Fish and Wildlife

Early in autumn, grouse are widely scattered. Be prepared to walk miles of leafy uplands to find a few birds.

season for the simple purpose of relieving excess energy. While others believe that ruffed grouse drum in autumn to declare to young dispersing birds that a territory is already claimed. Zero in on the thumping of wings and the benefit is obvious—you know at least one grouse is nearby!

If hunting with a dog, signal it in close. Approach the drumming spot as quietly as possible, stopping frequently with shotgun ready, anticipating the flush of a nervous grouse. But be advised that this technique will not always yield a grouse. A cock bird, knowing that predators often stalk his drumming, is instinctively spooky and might well have departed upon hearing your approach.

While covering miles upon miles of beautiful, blazing uplands is a grand experience, the pursuit of ruffed grouse in early autumn can be frustrating. With leaves still clinging to the trees, simply seeing, much less shooting, a flushing grouse can be a major accomplishment. Putting up 10 to 15 birds (a great day of grouse hunting anywhere) and shooting at but one or two is not uncommon.

Again, a well-trained pointing dog can be invaluable, pinning

Photo by Michael Hanback

Young grouse often sit nicely for pointing dogs like English setters early in the season.

birds that you must shoot before they vanish 15 yards into a canopy of leaves. When hunting with or without a dog you can increase your early-season shooting opportunities by employing this technique. Leave the dense woods and walk logging roads, field edges, power cuts, any sliver of opening that provides a window of visibility. If hunting solo, walk slowly and pause frequently. If you have a dog along, have it quarter into the bordering edge cover. When birds roar across or through tiny keyholes in the leafy timber, the gunning will be challenging. But at least you

Photo by Michael Hanback

The brushy edges of logging roads are excellent places to find ruffed grouse anytime of season.

may enjoy a split-second to snap shoot at a bird against open, blue sky.

Late-Season Techniques

In the North ruffed grouse seasons may close in November. Down South, seasons run through December, January, into February in some states. Regardless of where and when you grouse hunt, going late in the season offers a major advantage. The birds have begun to concentrate where late-autumn and winter forage is abundant. Ruffs, sometimes found in pairs or even small coveys of three to six (particularly in winter) seek herbs, leaves, buds and to a lesser extent fruits in prime covers. And with the leaves down and the thinnest understory toppled by heavy frosts, these covers are obvious. The grouse hunter can stand before a sprawl-ing piece of country and easily spot likely grouse areas.

Look for all the classic edges, of course. Be sure to hunt the fringes of fields, clearcuts and streams, as you did earlier in the season. Also seek out the densest tangles of alder, mountain laurel or other low-growing shrubbery in the area. Hunt every deadfall

Photo by Joe Workosky

After a fresh snow, look for three-toed tracks wending amid thickets. You can often follow, flush and bag a grouse.

structure in sight. Such places are preferred loafing spots in late autumn.

Hunting these areas with a pointing dog is again advantageous. With dew or frost upon the ground, scenting conditions are prime. And in and around dense alder, laurel and deadfalls grouse often hold well for a dog.

Shoot a grouse late in the season and you should check the bird's crop. This tells you precisely what the grouse has recently eaten. Often a grouse's crop will be stuffed with one preferred bud or leaf. Determine this and you can further concentrate your hunting in areas teeming with this choice food.

In the coldest weather, concentrate your hunting on south-facing hillsides, draws, valleys and stream bottoms, where grouse move to feed and loaf in the subtle winter sun. On the coldest days, don't hunt too early. In freezing or stormy weather, grouse may remain roosted the better part of a morning. Wait until later in the day, when the grouse are moving about in sunlit edges and emitting scent, to put your dogs into the cover.

Hunting grouse in snow cover can be fun and effective. Ruffs, like most gamebirds, are spooky in snow, their protective natural camouflage negated by the canvas of white. But you know where they are likely to be — loafing in conifer fringes or laurel tangles, nipping buds in stands of hardwood saplings, scratching for fruits on south-facing hillsides and clearcut fringes where the winter sun has melted patches of snow. Find grouse in these areas, get lucky enough to flush them in range, and the shooting can be

Photo by Michael Hanback

Late in the season, hunt along south-facing hillsides, hollows and stream bottoms. You should be able to find a grouse or two feeding and loafing in subtle winter sunlight.

superb — the gray or brown birds are easily picked up amid the leafless trees and backdrop of white.

In freshly fallen snow, you can also track grouse, as you would deer. Look for three-toed tracks in a straight line (grouse place one foot directly in front of the other when walking). Seek grouse tracks wending below the thickest shrubbery or conifer edges you can find; the birds must walk hidden from airborne predators. Follow the birds and peer not only over the tops of the cover, as you would all season, but up into treetops as well. In a snowy winter covert, a ruff may explode from beneath the snow or out of a shallow snow depression or sail from a conifer perch.

Finally, if seasons run into late winter in your area, never overhunt a cover. Winter is a critical time for ruffed grouse. Shoot a bird or two and leave the remainder in hope that they will survive the elements to breed in springtime. As with most upland gamebirds, studies have shown that hunting has an inconclusive or negligible effect on overall grouse populations from year to year. It behooves us all to hunt smartly and ethically. We should show the utmost respect for this grand gamebird, doing our part to ensure healthy grouse populations for years to come.

Where to Go

The ruffed grouse is the number one gamebird in Michigan, Wisconsin and Minnesota. In the Northeast, Maine, New York, Pennsylvania and West Virginia offer fine gunning. In the Southeast, western Virginia reports good hunting (grouse are hunted with varying degrees of success in mountainous areas farther south as well). Idaho and Washington offer good gunning, though the ruffed grouse is largely underhunted out West. Grouse hunting can be excellent throughout Canada, with New Brunswick, Manitoba, Alberta and British Columbia offering top opportunities.

Photo by Rob Seas

The ruffed grouse is America's most popular and widespread native upland gamebird.

CHAPTER 11

WESTERN GROUSE

In addition to the ruffed grouse, six grouse of various sizes, colors, demeanors and habitats range across western and northwestern North America. They are the sharp-tailed, sage, blue and spruce grouse. In addition, they include the prairie chicken and ptarmigan. These western grouse can be divided into two categories:

- **Prairie Grouse**
- **Mountain Grouse**

For the upland gunner, the prairie grouse, particularly the sharp-tailed and sage, provide the lion's share of wingshooting opportunities. Western grouse range extensively across western plains and grasslands, being relatively abundant in peak years. These birds possess fine sporting qualities. They are sharp-eyed, wary and unpredictable, either running or flushing wildly from

Photo Courtesy North Dakota Game and Fish Department

Historical records show the prairie region held phenomenal numbers of prairie chickens before the plow turned the vast amounts of grasslands into agricultural land.

hunters and dogs. On the wing, sharptails and chickens are fast, strong fliers, rising swiftly and skimming low over the horizon. And what wonderfully diverse gunning sage grouse provide! The big, long-winged birds lumber up like young wild turkeys. They fascinate, and often freeze and unnerve, the unsuspecting shotgunner.

Then there are the mountain grouse, interesting products of their wilderness environments. Seldom seeing and encountering humans in remote, rugged mountain habitats, blue grouse and spruce grouse and ptarmigan often become tight-sitting "fool hens." But hunting these species has special appeal, taking you into beautiful, secluded, peaceful uplands. As further reward, a bag of mountain birds will prove delicious on the table at camp or home.

THE PRAIRIE GROUSE

Three of the western grouse, the sharp-tailed and sage grouse and prairie chicken, are true prairie grouse, inhabiting sprawling plains and grasslands.

Photo by Michael Hanback

Walking miles of wide-open spaces without seeing another hunter is one of the most alluring aspects of pursuing western grouse.

Range

The sharp-tailed grouse, *Pedioecetes phasianellus*, has proved the most adaptable and resilient of North American prairie grouse. Once a bird of sprawling, virgin grasslands, the sharptail has adapted to modern, broken agricultural habitat. The species now thrives in extensive northern brushlands as well. Today, sharptails range from Wyoming and Nebraska north through the Dakotas, Minnesota, Wisconsin, Montana and Idaho. They are found across all of Alberta, Saskatchewan and Manitoba, into north-central Canada, ranging as far north as central Alaska.

Source: **Grouse and Quails of North America,** *Johnsgard*

Range of Prairie Grouse

■ Sharp-tailed
■ Sage
■ Prairie Chicken

The sage grouse, *Centrocercus urophasianus*, is a hardy Western native, seemingly found wherever there is extensive sagebrush. This includes a huge chunk of real estate from New Mexico and Colorado north through Wyoming and Montana. They range into southern Alberta and Saskatchewan, west through Idaho,

Washington and Oregon, and south through California, Nevada and Utah.

Two huntable prairie chickens, the greater, *Tympanuchus cupido*, and lesser, *Tympanuchus pallidicinctus*, inhabit the United States. A third prairie chicken, the Attwater's, *Tympanuchus cupido attwateri*, is not currently hunted. While chickens were once far-ranging and abundant, their range and numbers are limited today. Unlike the sharptail, the prairie chickens have not flourished where native grasslands have fallen to the plow.

Today, chickens are confined to scattered pockets of grasslands across the Midwest and West. The greater prairie chicken, most abundant of the two huntable species, inhabits pockets in the following states: North and South Dakota, Nebraska, Kansas, Oklahoma, Texas, Minnesota, Wisconsin and Michigan. The lesser chicken is a bird of the southern Great Plains, residing in varying numbers in Colorado, Kansas, Oklahoma, Texas and New Mexico.

Biology and Behavior

Sharp-tailed grouse are 15 to 20 inches long and weigh approximately two pounds. They are gray-black-brown birds flecked with white. Their fluffy breasts are white with vertical brown markings. Their white-rimmed, pointed tails give the species its name.

Cock birds have a yellow to orange comb (the erectile tissue varies in color with a bird's mood) over each eye, and inflatable purple air sacs on their necks. Like all western grouse, these combs and air sacs are most prominent during spring breeding displays.

Sharptails inhabit a variety of terrains today: prairies, grasslands, brushlands and shelterbelts rimming croplands. The birds glean berries, rose hips, grasses and seeds, and browse willow, birch and poplar leaves and buds. They feed readily upon spilled wheat, oats, barley and other grains. Between feedings and at night, sharptails loaf and roost on the ground.

Like many Western grouse, the sharptail performs an elaborate courtship ritual each spring. Cocks gather on dancing grounds, called leks, where they raise their tails and wings, inflate their air sacs and "boom" to attract hens and challenge other males. From April to June, hens lay five to 16 olive-brown eggs and incubate them in 3½ weeks.

Sharptails are strong runners, often eluding predators by

Photo by Leonard Lee Rue

Sharp-tailed grouse are buff birds flecked in black and white. On leks, males lift their pointed tails, spread their wings, inflate their air sacs and "boom" to attract females.

Photo by Judd Cooney

The sage grouse, 30 inches long and weighing up to six pounds, is the largest grouse in North America. In spring, males balloon air sacs on their chests and fan their spiked tails to lure hens.

scurrying into thick cover. Once they flush, rising with a "cuk-cuk-cuk" calling, the streamlined birds are one of the swiftest flying grouse, twisting away up to 30 mph, often sailing easily a mile or more before setting down.

The sage grouse, commonly referred to as "sage hen" out West, is the largest North American grouse. Males measure up to 30 inches long and weigh 5 to 6 pounds. Females are considerably smaller, typically weighing 3 to 5 pounds. Both sexes are grayish-brown with white breasts, and have long, pointed, spike-like tail feathers.

Sagebrush is the lifeline of this hardy western grouse. Sage hens feed heavily on the leaves and shoots of sage. They use their impeccable natural camouflage to hide easily amid the dusky, gray-green brush.

Sage grouse perform the most spectacular courtship ritual of all North American game birds. In spring, cock birds, sometimes in groups of 10 to 100, return to traditional leks to balloon the yellowish air sacs on their chests, fan their spiked tails and dance suggestively to attract hens. Receptive hens yield to copulation, then nest under a sage bush. Sage grouse hens lay 7 to 13 green, spotted eggs, which hatch in about 27 days.

In early autumn, sage grouse are often found in small groups of five or six birds. But it is not uncommon to run across huge flocks. When pursued, sage hens will either fly or run ahead of dogs and hunters. When flushing, they lumber up, clucking deeply, then dip and level off, flying 25 mph with a tail wind.

The greater prairie chicken is about 18 inches long and weighs two pounds. The bird is "barred" with an impressive array of

Photo by Len Rue, Jr.

Photo by Leonard Lee Rue III

Both greater and lesser prairie chickens appear virtually identical. But look close — the greater (right) is a tad larger and more vividly barred than the lesser.

brown and tan horizontal patterns. It has a short, rounded tail. Both sexes feature long, black pinnate feathers on each side of the neck, hence the formal name pinnated grouse. Like sharptails, male prairie chickens have orange-yellow combs over each eye and inflatable neck sacs. The lesser prairie chicken closely mirrors the greater, yet is smaller and less vividly barred and colored.

Both chickens inhabit areas with vast reaches of virgin grasslands and prairies. Here, the birds feed upon the leaves, seeds and fruits of native grasses, weeds, plants and flowers. Chickens also travel to nearby grainfields to feed upon sorghum, corn, oats, wheat and rye.

On spring mornings, male chickens gather on short-grass prairies to dance and attract hens. Like sharptails, they inflate their air sacs and boom loudly. Males jump and flutter and often fight fiercely over territory and females. After copulation, hens lay 10 to 13 eggs in grass-lined nests and hatch them in 24 days.

Prairie Grouse Hunting Tactics

Similar in behavior, sharp-tailed grouse and prairie chickens are often hunted with the same basic strategy.

Begin by tailoring your hunting to the time of day. Both prairie grouse follow the feed-early, rest-at-midday and feed-late routine. In early morning and late afternoon, hunt the edges of harvested stubble fields and grasslands. Many hunters take a strategic stand and glass the wide-open countryside with binoculars, looking for the bobbing heads of feeding grouse amid the stubble or short grass.

If sharptails or chickens are traveling from great distances to feed upon spilled grain, you can often experience fine pass-shooting as the birds wing into a prime stubble field. With this technique, hunting effectively often hinges on patterning the incoming grouse for a day or two, then setting up strategically in their flight path at dawn.

From midmorning to mid-afternoon, hunt fence lines, shelterbelts, ravines and ditches for loafing birds. This is when one discernible difference between sharptails and prairie chickens becomes evident. While sharptails can be found loafing in thickly brushed shelterbelts, overgrown fencelines and strips of heavy brushland, chickens prefer resting in tall-grass fields, swales, draws and ditches.

During the day, two or three hunters spaced along a narrow

Photo Courtesy North Dakota Game and Fish Department

During midday, a good place to hunt loafing sharptails is in thick, brushy draws, ravines and shelterbelts.

strip of security cover, marching along and covering all sides and escape routes, is a good technique. Prairie grouse are notorious for scurrying from a dog or hunter, running to the opposite side of a shelterbelt or fence row before flushing unseen. Covering all angles leads to more shooting.

Regardless of when and where you go, never pass up the opportunity to hunt around an abandoned homestead or ranch building, or a working grain elevator, silo or storage shed. These prominent features in flat, sprawling prairie grouse country are magnets for the birds. Typically rimmed with rose hips and other shrubbery as well as willow, birch or poplar saplings, remnant outbuildings and their surrounding cover provide good security and a variety of natural foods for both sharptails and chickens. Grain elevators and storage sheds provide abundant spilled grain after the late-summer harvest, drawing prairie grouse in bunches.

Speaking of bunches, sharptails are often found in groups of four, six, perhaps eight birds in September and early October. These birds, many young of the year, will often hold reasonably well for a pointing dog. Later in the season, huge flocks of sharptails, some numbering 50 to 100 birds, may be encountered. These wild, spooky grouse in sprawling country are tough on pointing dogs. Make sure your dog works close and under control

Photo by Michael Hanback

Hunt around abandoned homesteads and ranch buildings. Cover and food sources rimming these structures draw sharptails and prairie chickens like magnets.

Photo Courtesy Outdoor Oklahoma

Early morning and late afternoon, are excellent for hunting feeding prairie chickens along edges of stubble fields and grasslands.

at all times, or hunt with a close-working flusher or nonslip retriever.

Being less dependent upon a feeding-loafing schedule, sage grouse can be found anytime of day amid the endless seas of sagebrush. Obviously, then, the first key to hunting effectively for the big gray birds is to narrow down the expansive country with hopes of concentrating your hunting in prime locations.

There are several ways to do this. First is to glass from a high vantage point, looking for feeding or loafing birds. This can, however, be tough to do. Unlike sharptails, sage hens do not fly or walk into feeding areas, but mingle anywhere in the vast prairie. Because of that grayish natural camouflage, they can be exceedingly difficult to see.

If you cannot find birds with your binoculars, look for breaks in the rolling prairie — draws, gullies, swales, ravines, knolls, roadside ditches, ridges, flats, plateaus. Sage grouse often linger in and around such terrain features, perhaps to break the strong prairie wind or to seek suitable cover from predators. Mentally mark several such terrain features and strike out across the prairie to hunt them.

Photo by Michael Hanback

When fanning out across sage grouse country, be sure to zero in on prominent draws, gullies, ditches and plateaus. Birds linger in and around such terrain features, which offer abundant food and shelter from prairie winds and predators.

If hunting on a working farm or ranch, where fields of alfalfa meet seas of sage, hunt these edges. While most sage hens are indeed shot in the sage, grouse will flock to harvested alfalfa edges when available.

Also, seek out stock tanks, ponds, creeks and springs in the area. On the most arid prairies, sage grouse will be found feeding within a mile of water. If water is particularly scarce, grouse may fly in from long distances to water early each morning or late each afternoon. If this is the case, you may be treated to some of the most unique pass-shooting in North America as the big bomber-like birds cruise in to drink.

Photo by Judd Cooney

On arid prairies, you can find sage grouse watering at seeps, creeks, ponds and stock tanks.

Photo by Michael Hanback

Sage grouse, with highly effective gray camouflage, often sit extremely tight. It takes persistent zigzagging to flush and shoot a couple of birds.

When hunting water-holes, or any prime stretches of sage for that matter, search for large, chicken-like tracks in the sand and mud, and also for the sage grouse's distinctive droppings — silver-dollar-sized splotches the color and texture of congealed motor oil. Fresh droppings and tracks tell you sage grouse are using the area, and that you should scour the nearby sage thoroughly.

This is best done by either circling or zigzagging out from the water source, draw or plateau. Hunt first in small patterns, then fan out in increasingly large coverages. Sage grouse, often found in small groups of four to eight birds, may scurry away just in front of a hunter or dogs or sit tightly in hopes danger will pass. A pointing dog can serve you well, but a close-working flusher or retriever is most common in sage country. It often requires persistent, painstaking walking to put the big birds into the air.

When they flush, you are in for a real treat. Most likely the birds will stagger up, two here, one there, then one more. It takes them awhile to get off the ground, which gives you plenty of time to run at them, aim and shoot (remember to use caution with this technique). If the birds flush well within shotgun range, they are not particularly hard to hit, but if they flush wild and get a head of steam their large size and slow wing beats can be deceptive, causing the upland gunner to miscalculate lead and shoot behind birds. As with any type of upland birds large or small, remember that you must lead adequately to fold angling sage grouse cleanly and consistently.

Because their ranges overlap, combining a bird hunt for sage grouse (or perhaps even sharptails, pheasants and Hungarian partridge) and antelope is a popular and exciting October adventure. You can hire an outfitter or arrange the hunt yourself for this bird-big game combo. Much of the finest pronghorn and

Photo Courtesy North Dakota Game and Fish Department

When a sage grouse gets up a head of steam, its large size and slow wing beats can be deceptive, causing you to shoot behind. Be sure to lead angling birds adequately at long ranges.

sage grouse hunting in Wyoming, Montana and other western states is on BLM land. There are rewards aplenty. The western weather is typically pleasant in early autumn. In a prime area, successfully stalking a nice antelope buck is a three-day affair at most. Then, perhaps having brought your gundog along, you can spend three or four days enjoying the fun and unique bird hunting the prairie has to offer.

Where to Go

In peak population years, Montana and the Dakotas offer some of the finest sharptail hunting in the United States. The southern plains of Alberta, Saskatchewan and Manitoba have long been recognized as top covers for sharptails.

For sage grouse, Montana, Wyoming, southern Idaho, Colorado and Utah offer good to excellent hunting.

As compared to other western grouse, limited hunting opportunities exist for prairie chickens today. Best bets for greater chickens include eastern Kansas, Nebraska and South Dakota. Hunting for lessers is confined to pockets in Oklahoma, Kansas and New Mexico.

THE MOUNTAIN GROUSE

Among the western grouse, the blue and spruce grouse and ptarmigan are considered mountain grouse because they frequent high alpine terrains and conifer forests.

Range

The blue grouse, *Dendragapus obscurus*, is the most wide-ranging and accessible of the western mountain grouse. It dwells from the alpines of New Mexico, Nevada and California north through Colorado, Wyoming, Montana, Idaho, Oregon and Washington, into British Columbia, western Alberta and the Yukon.

The spruce grouse, *Canachites canadensis*, is a bird of the northern conifer forests. It is common from Alaska east across northern Canada. In the United States the spruce inhabits high country in Oregon, Idaho, Montana and Wyoming and, interestingly, as far east as Minnesota, Wisconsin and Michigan.

Three species of ptarmigan—white-tailed, rock, *Lagopus mutus,* and willow, *Lagopus lagopus*, (the latter the state bird of Alaska) inhabit the Northwest. Most wide-ranging and accessible to North

Source: Grouse and Quails of North America, *Johnsgard*

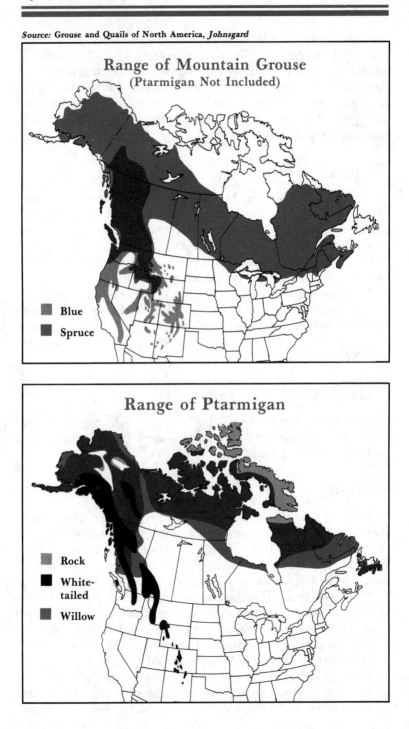

Photo by Judd Cooney

A male blue grouse has a dull, bluish-gray body, but its eye combs, inflatable air sacs and light-tipped tail are distinctive.

American sportsmen is the white-tailed ptarmigan, *Lagopus leucurus*. The white-tailed ptarmigan ranges from southern Alaska south across British Columbia, into Washington, Montana, Wyoming, Colorado and New Mexico.

Biology and Behavior

Blue grouse are 15 to 20 inches long and weigh two to 2½ pounds. Males are dull, bluish-gray, hence the common name dusky or sooty grouse. The males also have a yellow to red comb over each eye and air sacs on the neck. Females are mottled brown. Both sexes have a square, dark-gray tail.

In the mountainous West, the blue grouse migrates seasonally from low to high country. In spring, blues gather on low slopes in relatively open woodlands, where males court hens, strutting and inflating their air sacs. Hens lay 7 to 10 buff-colored eggs in a ground nest, and incubate the clutch in 26 days.

Blue grouse remain on low slopes spring through summer, feeding upon insects, berries, leaves and flowers. Come fall, these gray birds move uphill (contrary to most mountain game, which migrates down to lower elevations in winter) into high conifer forests and the edges of alpine parks. The winter diet of blue grouse consists heavily of spruce, fir and pine needles and buds.

*Photo Courtesy Quebec
Department of Recreation, Fish and Game*

The spruce grouse is solitary and tight-sitting, the true "fool hen" of northern coniferous forests.

Blue grouse are loners, often traveling singly or in small groups. When disturbed, they simply walk or scurry from potential danger, or flush into a nearby conifer tree.

Spruce grouse are smaller than blues, 15 to 17 inches long and weighing one to 1½ pounds. Males are grayish-black with white-spotted sides and red eye combs. Females are drab brown.

Spruce grouse inhabit northern coniferous forests. Often tree dwellers, the birds feed on the needles and buds of spruce, jack pine and fir trees. The birds eat the leaves and seeds of herbaceous plants if available.

Like blue grouse, spruce males strut and display for hens in spring. From May to July, females lay five to 10 pinkish eggs in a depression under conifer limbs. The eggs hatch in 23 to 24 days.

Spruce grouse are solitary and even more tight-sitting than blue grouse. For this reason, the bird is the true "fool hen" of the Northwest.

The white-tailed ptarmigan, smallest of North American grouse, is a foot long and weighs a pound or less. Interestingly, it is the only grouse to change feather color to match seasonal habitat. During summer, ptarmigan are rust brown with white wings, tails and undersides. In winter, the birds turn pure white to blend with the omnipresent snow.

The white-tailed ptarmigan is a true alpine dweller, often found at elevations of 10,000 feet or more. In the high country, the birds feed upon the catkins, buds and leaves of alder, willow, birch and poplar, and the needles and buds of spruce and fir.

The white-tailed variety is the only ptarmigan that nests in

Photos by
Charles Summers, Jr./Rue Enterprises

The white-tailed ptarmigan is the only grouse to change feather color to match seasonal habitat. In summer birds are brown; in winter they turn white to blend with snow.

the lower 48 states. Hens lay 4 to 16 reddish-buff eggs in June or July and incubate them in about 23 days.

Ptarmigan are more gregarious than blue or spruce grouse. Coveys of 10 to 20 or upwards of 30 to 50 birds are not uncommon during fall hunting season.

Mountain Grouse Hunting Tactics

In autumn, living in high mountains with mule deer, elk, goats and sheep, blue and spruce grouse are often shot incidentally "for the pot" by big game hunters. The birds provide delectable camp fare when shot and cared for properly.

Some hunters head-shoot grouse with their big game rifles. This presents two potential problems. First, rifle shots can spook big game, particularly elk. If you shoot an inch or two low, you destroy the grouse and any chance for a delicious camp dinner.

When "side-hunting" mountain grouse on a big game hunt, it's wise to pack a .22 pistol or rifle or a shotgun into camp and use this for "potting" a bird or two. This is quieter, safer and much more likely to save the breast meat.

If you are bowhunting deer or elk, shooting grouse is practical, fun and excellent field practice. While a broadhead-tipped arrow can be effective, many archers carry a shaft or two tipped with a blunt, judo or other small game head. These heads provide effective killing shock for grouse. They also inhibit shaft velocity and will not embed in trees, making arrows easy to find and retrieve.

Photo by Judd Cooney

Hunters often shoot mountain grouse "for the pot" while pursuing elk or mule deer. Bowhunting the tight-sitting birds is challenging and excellent field practice.

While only a minority of western wingshooters do it, hunting mountain grouse, with or without a dog, can be fun and rewarding. The real challenge lies in hiking the mountains, getting up into the birds' autumn habitat. Once there, hunt the edges of parks, snow slides and meadows, zigzagging into the omnipresent spruce, fir or pine forest. While mountain grouse are scattered all over the high country, they often congregate in fringes. Spot a blue or spruce grouse and you will often have to run

Photo by Judd Cooney

Walk the edges of parks, snow slides and meadows, then hunt 100 yards or so back in adjoining spruce and pine forest. You should bag a blue grouse or two.

at the bird to flush it. At times like this, a flushing dog can be a big help. Then, hammering half as loudly as a ruffed grouse, a spruce or blue will often helicopter up into the nearest tree. Holding your shotgun in one hand, throw rocks or sticks at the grouse. Eventually it will fly, nine times out of 10 sailing downhill through thick conifers, where the shooting can be fast and tricky.

In early fall, ptarmigan are often found in mountain valleys and river bottoms, mingling at mid-slope in willow and alder thickets. If snow cover is late, an effective technique is to gain a strategic vantage point and scan or glass slopes for winter-white birds; they are easily spotted against brown grass and gray shale. Hunting coveys of ptarmigan under these circumstances often provides sporty wingshooting. Under these circumstances the birds are skittish and prone to fly, as if realizing their snow camouflage is working against them.

Photo by Leonard Lee Rue III

If snow cover comes late to ptarmigan country, gain a strategic vantage and glass. Winter-white birds are easily spotted against brown grass and rocks.

Don't get the idea that all mountain grouse are tight-sitting pushovers. Like all North American grouse, blues, spruce and ptarmigan are unpredictable. Some fly extraordinarily well, especially in accessible areas where they are regularly flushed by big game hunters, hikers, horsemen or hardy upland hunters. Here, the mountain birds can provide fast-paced wingshooting.

Where to Go

Hundreds of thousands of blue and spruce grouse and ptarmigan are bagged by hunters each autumn. The mountain-dwelling birds are widely scattered and reclusive, often shot incidentally by big game hunters. Therefore, gathering accurate population and harvest figures is difficult for upland bird biologists. Suffice to say that most high-country, coniferous forests within these species' ranges, from Colorado to Oregon to western Canada to Alaska, should harbor enough grouse for fair to excellent hunting.

Chapter 12

Woodcock

Photo by Maslowski

The American woodcock, a chunky little game bird with big, dark eyes and a long, pointed bill, is a favorite of upland gunners east of the Mississippi River.

As the shuffling of feet draws nearer, the chunky little game bird, the color of fallen oak leaves, presses tightly into the moist forest floor, its big brown eyes scanning the creek bottom for danger. Into the sun-mottled cover prances a black-ticked setter, moving left and right, suddenly freezing, casting its ominous shadow mere feet over the quivering bird. The hunter, dressed in tweeds and canvas and cradling a fine 20-gauge side-by-side, eases in, until the bird helicopters upward, twittering into the treetops, dangling in midair, its long-billed silhouette etched against the brilliant autumn sun. The bird then dances amid the

185

oak and hickory tops, weaving and fluttering erratically, offering no shot but spiraling to earth a mere 50 yards away, where setter and hunter mark a line and again take up the glorious October pursuit.

Such a unique fellow, the American woodcock. What pure pleasure to hunt. Inhabiting easy-to-walk bottomland cover, this shorebird turned uplander can be found by the hundreds when migrations are on. Then, sitting tightly, the birds hold well for pointing dogs. And that whirling, twirling, twittering flight! Just bizarre and erratic enough to make the close-range gunning zesty and unpredictable. Little wonder this odd-looking, odd-behaving game bird has long been a favorite of upland shotgunners east of the Mississippi River.

Range

The woodcock, *Scolopax minor*, is a migratory game bird of the eastern half of the United States. The U. S. Fish and Wildlife Service recognizes two woodcock populations, the Central and Atlantic flights. Combined, these populations summer across the central and northeastern United States, from Tennessee north to Maine, west to Minnesota and into Canada. Woodcock winter across the Southeast, from Virginia south to Florida, west to Arkansas and eastern Texas.

Biology and Behavior

The woodcock, or timberdoodle, is 10 to 12 inches long. Males weigh six ounces; females are slightly heavier. This is a stocky bird feathered brown, tan and black—perfect natural camouflage for the bogs and hardwood bottoms it inhabits. Woodcock have big, bulging eyes. Most distinctive are their long, slender bills, up to 3 inches in length.

Woodcock prefer moist or marshy woodlands, fields, thickets and stream and river bottoms. When such habitat freezes over in autumn, the birds migrate south, often in large numbers, moving at the same time, but individually and at night. They fly in vigorous spurts to find the nearest moist, unlocked earth.

The bulk of the woodcock's diet is earthworms. The birds typically feed early in the morning and at dusk, probing the boggy ground with their bills.

Woodcock perform a sensational courtship flight in spring called a peent. On their dancing, or singing, grounds males strut, then

Source: Management of Migratory Shore and Upland Game Birds, *Sanderson (Editor)*

Range of American Woodcock

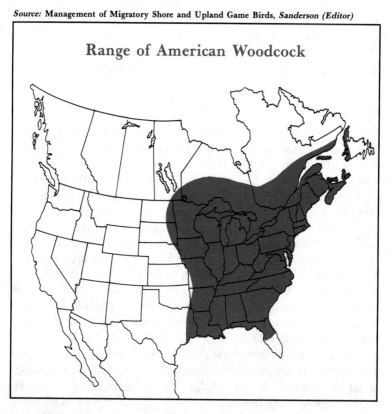

Photo by Maslowski

Earthworms are the bulk of the woodcock's diet. Chicks learn early to bore their bills into moist bottomland habitat for food.

helicopter upward and return to earth in a fluttering spiral, twittering all the while. Females attracted to this flight are bred by the cock birds. From March to May, hens lay four buff-colored eggs in a shallow depression and hatch them in 20 days.

Woodcock Hunting Tactics

It's possible that hunters can find resident birds throughout the woodcock's range almost anytime of year. However, the best woodcock hunting in North America is tied to the birds' annual autumn migration. Indeed, much woodcock hunting is boom or bust. When flight birds are in, a hunter may find dozens of woodcock in a prime cover, offering excellent shooting for a day or two. Before the birds arrive and after they leave, the cover will be barren, except, perhaps, for a resident bird or two.

What constitutes prime woodcock cover? It should be moist, but not wet. These shorebirds hate wading in water. Ideal habitat includes a creek or river bottom, boggy field or thicket or hardwood flat, anywhere the birds can drill their long bills for earthworms. Prime covers will have second-growth saplings and brushy, not grassy, understory.

There are regional habitat preferences. Up north, hunt woodcock in mixed forests of birch, aspen, and maple laced with soggy alder thickets. In the Mid-Atlantic and South, seek woodcock in damp, moist oak bottoms laced with greenbrier or blackberry tangles.

In many areas across the woodcock's range, the birds can be found alongside ruffed grouse, inhabiting damp thickets on the wintering range. Woodcock are often found near bobwhites, in hardwood bottoms and moist, overgrown fields.

How to hunt these covers? Since woodcock are on the move a lot, migrating at night, the only way to know if birds are in a cover is to walk it. Look for sign—chalky droppings with white centers and holes in mud flats where birds have drilled for earthworms. Finding no sign or woodcock, depart the cover, but hunt it several more times that season. Woodcock migrate in spurts, with birds often dropping into or leaving a cover overnight. A barren cover one morning may be teeming with dozens of timberdoodles the next. Once you find a cover woodcock are using, return next season, as birds often use the same migration stop overs annually.

Since woodcock feed most actively at dawn and dusk, hunt prime habitat early and late. During midday, try dry, sunlit

Photo by Mike Strandlund

Hunt woodcock in stream and river bottoms, boggy fields and thickets and adjoining woodland flats laced with second-growth saplings. A well-trained pointing dog helps locate the tight-sitting birds regardless of the terrain.

Photo by John Hall,
Vermont Department of Fish and Wildlife

hillsides, where woodcock often rest. These will be located only a short, spiraling flight from bottomland cover.

Hunt with a pointing dog if possible. Setters are the all-time favorite woodcock dogs, but pointers and Brits are effective, of course. Close-hunting flushers, such as cocker or springer spaniels, are super woodcock companions. Not only will a dog add pleasure to your hunting, it will allow you to double your finds. Hunt alone and you will walk over dozens of tight-sitting birds.

189

Photo by Michael Hanback

A hunter without a dog can be successful by zigzagging bottomland cover, pausing frequently for 30 seconds at a time. This stop-and-go routine often unnerves tight-holding woodcock, causing them to helicopter up into the air.

A word on pointing dog work. While most dogs will point woodcock, some refuse to retrieve them, shunning their scent and the taste of their feathers. If you run into this problem and intend to hunt woodcock seriously, you can settle for the dog pointing dead birds that you then retrieve, or go the extra training mile and force-train your dog to retrieve.

If forced to hunt woodcock without a dog, you'll miss the beauty of stylish points and exciting flushes, but you can still be successful. Walk the covers as you would if hunting with a dog, zigzagging more to hit all the edges. Try the pause-and-go routine so common with dogless grouse hunters. Stopping frequently for 30 seconds to a minute at a time will often unnerve tight-sitting timberdoodles, causing them to helicopter up almost from beneath your boot soles.

Hunting with or without a dog, having flushed a woodcock and enjoying no shot or missing cleanly, follow up the flush immediately. Woodcock seldom fly far before sitting down again. Many fly only 100 yards or so, only to alight and sit tighter still the second time around.

Gunning Woodcock

The woodcock's close-range, whirling, up-and-down flight can cause gunning problems for hunters. Most missed birds are fired at too quickly, and then undershot.

When a woodcock flushes nearby, watch it while shouldering your shotgun. But resist the urge to shoot too quickly. Wait until the bird tops out in flight. In typical woodcock cover this would be at the tops of 10- to 30-foot second growth saplings. Then, shooting instinctively, simply blot out the bird and fire. Woodcock pause a millisecond at treetop height; put your shot charge of 8s or 9s there as it dangles in midair and you'll score. Be warned, however, not to wait until a woodcock levels the out across the treetops. Your target will be impossible to see and hit as it weaves and flutters through the cover. This is especially true during the early season when the leaves are still up.

Woodcock can also flush low and fast, providing grouse-like shooting especially along openings or forest edges.

Photo by Maslowski

Woodcock typically flush close but whirl up erratically. Waiting until the birds pause a second at treetops before shooting is one key to bagging your limit of timberdoodles.

Other Considerations

Woodcock hunters may also encounter the common snipe, *Capella gallinago*, along shorelines, flooded fields, and marsh edges. Snipe are not generally found under cover but prefer open areas. Like woodcock, snipe may sit tight while a hunter approaches but flush with a rapid zigzag flight before leveling off.

Although similar to a woodcock, the snipe is slightly smaller and slimmer. It is a striped brown and white bird with longer legs and longer, more pointed wings. Though small, snipe are excellent table fare, their meat resembling woodcock and dove in flavor and texture.

For more information on how to hunt snipe, see the second edition NRA Hunter Skills Series book, *Waterfowl Hunting*.

Where to Go

Top woodcock hunting areas in North America include northeastern Canada and the New England and Great Lakes states. Millions of woodcock winter in Louisiana, a late-year hot spot. Most any state in the woodcock's range can offer fair to excellent hunting, depending upon the unpredictable migrations and the quality of the cover.

CHAPTER 13
OTHER WESTERN UPLANDERS

Photo by Thomas C. Tabor

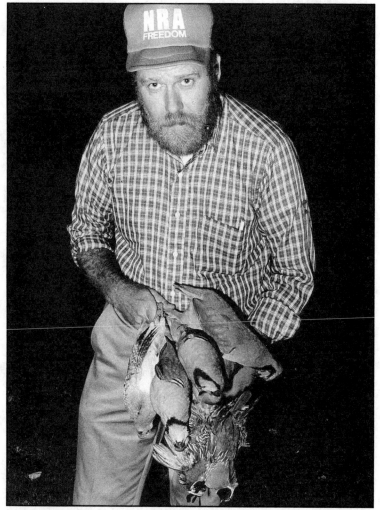

Chukars and Hungarian partridge can often be hunted alongside valley quail, providing the Western wingshooter an intriguing mixed bag.

I n addition to prairie and mountain grouse, and far west and desert quail, three unique gamebirds—a pair of imported partridge and a cousin of the barnyard pigeon—offer excellent Western wingshooting.

In many areas across the West today, there are a few other gamebirds that can be hunted alongside grouse and quail, providing fine mixed-bag shooting. They are:

- **Chukar**
- **Hungarian Partridge**
- **Band-tailed Pigeon**

Each of these other uplanders flies high on its own merits, for each is a sporty, challenging target. Whether hiking steep slopes for chukars, wading sprawling grasslands for Hungarians or pass-shooting bandtails in a high mountain saddle, pleasures aplenty await shotgunners beneath the big, arid skies.

THE CHUKAR

The chukar is one of the most physically challenging upland birds to hunt. Often success means hiking for miles along steep slopes to bag a few birds.

Range

The chukar, *Alectoris chukar*, was imported from Eurasia in the late 1800s. While chukars were introduced widely across the United States, the birds gained a foothold in the arid, rugged Northwest. Today, chukars are concentrated in Nevada, Utah, Oregon, Washington and Idaho. Populations exist in Montana, Wyoming, Colorado, Arizona, New Mexico and California as well. In Canada, chukars can be found in British Columbia. Chukars are also a favorite on hunting preserves in most areas.

Biology and Behavior

Chukars are 12 to 15 inches long and weigh one to 1½ pounds. They are striking gray birds, with black-barred flanks. Their buff-colored faces feature distinctive black stripes. The chukar's beauty is accentuated by crimson eye rings, bills and legs.

Chukars inhabit rugged mountains, often living as high as 10,000 feet. The birds prefer dry, rocky, sage- or cheatgrass-covered slopes, where they glean the seeds and fruits of low-lying plants.

Source: Grouse and Quails of North America, *Johnsgard*

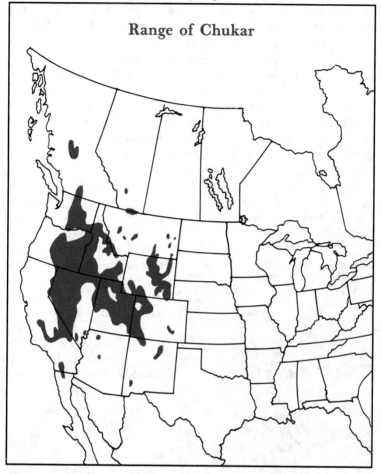

Range of Chukar

Chukars nest in rocks, with hens laying 10 to 20 cream-colored eggs in a grass-lined depression. Chicks hatch in 24 days.

Chukars are typically found in coveys of 10 to 20 birds. When spooked, chukars are notorious for running swiftly uphill to the peak of a ridge. Then, uttering a distinctive "chuk-chuk-chu-kar" call for which the species is named, the birds flush and sail down the opposite slope.

Chukar Hunting Tactics

Hardy bird hunters must hike and climb for hours and miles to find birds scattered over steep, rugged mountains. Upon locating a covey, the hunter is witness to the inhospitable behavior of chukars. Often standing helplessly out of shotgun range, the hunter can only watch as a covey scurries uphill before flushing wildly and flying strongly down an inaccessible slope.

Successful chukar hunting begins with locating birds in sprawling mountain habitat. In the arid western high country, chukars often water early in a creek, river or spring bottom, then spend midmorning to mid-afternoon feeding steadily uphill on a cheatgrass-laced hillside. The best strategy, however, is not to hunt early near low-lying water and work your way up (you'll never catch up to strong-walking chukars this way), but to hike high to a ridgeline or rocky rim first thing in the morning. There, scan nearby thin-grass slopes for feeding birds (lightweight, compact binoculars are easy to carry and an excellent aid). Listen, too, for feeding chukars. Try to zero in on the birds' tell-tale calling.

Photo by Neil Mishler

The chukar's black-barred face and flanks are distinctive. The birds reside on high, dry, grass-lined slopes.

If the day is hot and dry, as is often the case in early season, look for birds feeding and loafing on north-facing slopes and in cool, shady draws and basins. Hunt near a high-country water source if possible—the birds water daily, either early in the morning or before going to roost. Hunt a water hole for chukars as you would for western quail; walk around the pond, spring or creek, working your way out in widening circles to catch birds moving to and from water.

If the day is cold and snowy, seek chukars on sunlit south-facing slopes. Concentrate your hunting on melting, open patches of cheatgrass. While there, look for fresh chukar tracks in the snow and try sneaking quietly up on a covey.

If it's windy, chukars, like all upland birds, will be ultra-spooky. In the gale-force winds that often whip across chukar country,

Photo by Thomas C. Tabor

Chukars are one of the most challenging upland birds to hunt. You must often hike for miles in steep, rugged mountains to bag a bird or two.

check for birds in breeze-breaking draws and ravines and on the lee side of rock outcroppings.

Having located a covey of chukars, approach steadily and quietly from above or across the slope if possible. This will afford the best opportunity of cutting off birds if they run. As mentioned, hunt from below and you might never get a shot at chukars. They will simply outrace you uphill before flushing out of the country.

After flushing a covey, watch the birds closely. When you're hunting from above on open mountain slopes, the downhill flight of chukars is often easy to mark. Follow up quickly. Listen for the "chukara" assembly calling of scattered birds, which can lead you straight to singles. And often the singles sit tightly, offering fine shooting if you can find them.

To find chukars consistently, a well-trained pointing dog is an

Photo by Leonard Lee Rue III

Pointing dogs are an asset for cutting off running coveys of chukars, pinning tight-sitting singles and retrieving birds after the shot.

197

asset. A sharp pointer can cut off running chukar coveys, and help pin close-sitting singles. This can double your shooting.

Where to Go

While fair to good hunting can be found across the chukar's range, Washington, Oregon and Idaho consistently provide top gunning.

THE HUNGARIAN PARTRIDGE

The Hungarian patridge can be hunted on sprawling sage prairies or in agricultural stubble fields.

Range

The Hungarian partridge, *Perdix perdix*, was introduced into North America from Europe in the late 19th Century. While scattered pockets of birds inhabit northeastern and upper midwestern states, the Hungarian partridge has firmly established itself as a western species — major populations inhabit the Northwest and northern Great Plains. Hungarians range from Oregon, Washington and Idaho east across Montana, Wyoming and the Dakotas, into Minnesota. Southern Alberta, Saskatchewan and Manitoba are home to substantial numbers of Huns.

Photo Courtesy North Dakota Game and Fish Department

The Hungarian partridge is 12 inches long and weighs a pound. The rust-colored marking on the bird's belly is distinctive.

Source: Grouse and Quails of North America, *Johnsgard*

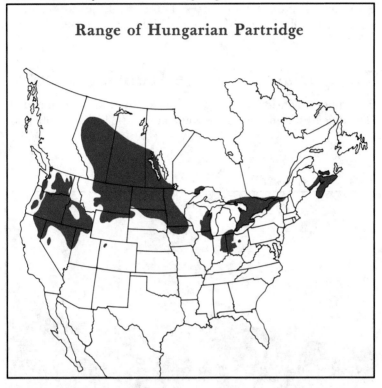

Range of Hungarian Partridge

Biology and Behavior

The Hungarian partridge, or simply Hun, is about 12 inches long and weighs a pound. Grayish-brown overall (hence its other common name, gray partridge) the birds feature tannish-orange faces and throats, along with distinctive rust-colored markings on their bellies.

Across much of its range, the Hun is considered a cropland bird. It uses agricultural areas extensively, feeding in stubble upon spilled wheat, corn, barley, oats and other grain. But the partridge is equally at home in sprawling grasslands and sage prairies, where it feeds mainly upon the seeds of wild plants.

Female huns nest in shallow, grass-lined depressions and lay 5 to 18 olive eggs. Chicks hatch in 25 days.

Hungarian partridge covey up like bobwhite quail, with 10 to 15 birds comprising a typical covey. The birds roost in short-grass

199

fields, either scattered or in a circle resembling the bobwhite's. As potential danger approaches, Huns sneak quickly through cover before flushing and sailing straight away at a moderately swift speed of about 35 mph.

Hungarian Partridge Hunting Tactics

Hunting Hungarian partridge is a lot like hunting bobwhite quail. The chief difference is where you look for the birds. While bob-

Photo by Mike Strandlund

In farm country, you can flush coveys of Huns from stubble fields and bordering grassy edges and draws.

whites often inhabit thick, brushy habitat today, Huns prefer relatively open, thin cover.

In agricultural areas, look for Huns in stubble fields and nearby edges, grassy fields and draws. Binoculars can be a great help in locating the bobbing heads of feeding birds. In wide-open grasslands, seek birds in draws, ravines and stream bottoms. On sage prairies, check for Huns in grassy draws and pockets and along grass-lined creek bottoms and shelter belts.

In these areas hunt Huns as you would bobwhites. Hunt feeding fields early in the morning and late in the day, when birds are most active. During midday, check loafing areas, likely nearby grass fields and draws. In afternoon, just prior to the evening feeding, Huns can often be found gleaning grit from ranch or prairie roads. The grassy ditches surrounding backcountry roads are excellent spots to find Huns all day long.

Another popular spot to hunt is the cover encircling an abandoned ranch building or homestead. Here, in addition to finding a covey of Huns, you can often run across sharptails. This offers a most rewarding mixed bag. Like sharptails and prairie chickens, Huns flock to crumbling structures amid sprawling, open country for the feeding and security cover they provide.

Photo by Michael Hanback

When hunting sprawling sage prairies, hit grassy draws, ravines and creek bottoms, and you'll likely shoot a couple of Hungarian partridge.

Along with thick shelterbelts, these areas also provide natural wind breaks on the plains. These are hot spots to hunt on windy days.

Huns are more prolific runners than bobwhites. They scurry easily through the typically thin cover in front of dogs and hunters. For this reason, some hunters use close-working flushing breeds to put birds into the air. Pointing dogs, however, can work extremely well on Huns. This is particularly true early in the season when coveys are comprised of young, close-sitting birds. A well-trained setter, Brittany, shorthair or Drahthaar is a boon anytime of season in big country, covering lots of habitat and pinning running birds.

Upon finding Huns, whether approaching a covey you spotted yourself or slipping in behind a birdy gundog, walk quickly but as quietly and as inconspicuously as possible. Stalk the birds, using any draw, shelterbelt or other natural break in the country for concealment. Huns are spooky game birds. Coveys place themselves in open, short-grass country, where up to 15 pairs of sharp eyes are constantly peeled for predators. If you bust headlong toward a covey of Huns, the birds will likely run and flush wildly out of shotgun range.

Having flushed a covey of Huns, hopefully shooting a bird or two, mark the birds' flight as closely as possible. Instead of scattering in all directions when flushed and beelining for thick cover like bobwhites, Huns often sail off en masse before the covey sits down together in the middle of a wide-open field. Interestingly, flushed Huns will often head for a small knoll or rolling ridge, alighting just on the opposite rim of the terrain break. Sneak quietly up the hill and you might put up the covey in shooting range.

Early in the season, flushed Huns, even those shot at repeatedly, may fly several hundred yards before sitting down again. Later, Huns may fly close to a mile. And late in the season, when snow is on the ground, Huns will sometimes dive into a snow bank to elude predators, hunters and dogs. Remember this when following up a covey. Flushing Huns from a snow bank in an eruption of white powder would undoubtedly be one of the season's fondest wingshooting memories.

Where to Go

In the United States, Washington, Oregon, Idaho, Nevada, Montana, North and South Dakota and Minnesota offer fair to fine

Photo by Michael Hanback

A peculiar habit of Huns—flushed coveys tend to fly to a prominent knob or ridge and alight together on the far slope. Sneak strategically over the terrain break, and you might reflush the covey.

Hungarian partridge hunting from year to year, depending on local bird populations. In Canada, southern to central Alberta, Saskatchewan and Manitoba are tops for Hun shooting.

THE BAND-TAILED PIGEON

The band-tailed pigeon is found in huntable numbers in oak and mixed-pine forests.

Range

Band-tailed pigeons, *Columba fasciata*, are migratory game birds inhabiting two western regions. A coastal population of band-tails summers in British Columbia, Washington and northern Oregon, flying south to winter across coastal California, into Mexico. Resident bandtails live year-round in Oregon and California.

A major pigeon population inhabits the southwest as well. Chief range is Colorado south to extreme western Texas. While large numbers of southwestern bandtails migrate, resident birds can be found throughout this range, particularly in the southern reaches.

Source: Management of Migratory Shore and Upland Game Birds, *Sanderson (Editor)*

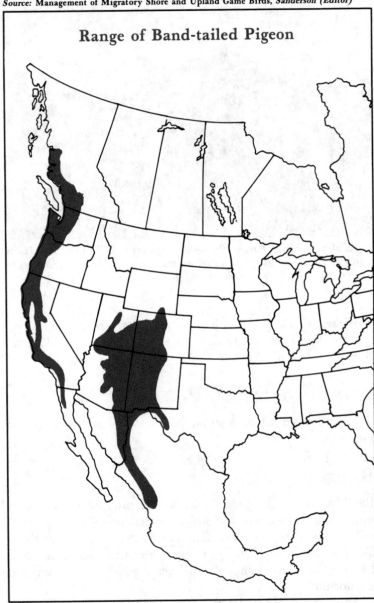

Range of Band-tailed Pigeon

Biology and Behavior

Band-tailed pigeons are noticeably larger than doves. The birds are 14 inches long and weigh nine to 12 ounces. Bluish-gray of body, the birds feature a gray band across the long, squared tail feathers, hence the species' name. Bandtails wear a narrow white band on the backs of their necks.

Unlike doves, band-tailed pigeons are woodland birds, inhabiting oak and mixed-pine forests. While these pigeons will glean grain if available, chief foods are nuts, berries and seeds.

Bandtails nest in trees from spring to late summer. Nesting in scattered colonies, females lay a single white egg that is incubated by both sexes in about 20 days.

These pigeons are often found in large flocks. The birds are exceptional fliers, leaping from danger on feeding grounds and flying swiftly and erratically through the forest habitat.

Band-tailed Pigeon Hunting Tactics

Hunting band-tailed pigeons is one of the most unique types of upland wingshooting in North America. It combines the fast-flying behavior of open-country birds with forested mountain habitat, creating an intriguing atmosphere in which to enjoy extremely challenging shooting.

Most bandtails are shot in hills and mountains, where hunters take stands in strategic saddles or passes and pass-shoot birds as they wing in to feed or water. Locating prime woodland feeding areas can be difficult — pigeon flocks scatter throughout the mountains to feed. Hunters should look for relatively open hillsides covered with oak, pinyon and other nut-bearing trees and shrubs. Mast crops fluctuate from year to year. Concentrate your hunting on hillsides where nuts are most abundant. Find a likely feeding ground, take a stand on a nearby point or in a pass that affords good visibility, then hunt early in the morning and late in the day for incoming birds.

Gunning watering holes, particularly in the arid Southwest, is an effective technique for pigeons. Ponds, creeks and springs are excellent hunting grounds early and late in the day, when the birds wing in to drink after feeding. Pigeons also have a natural affinity for salt licks. Find a salt lick near a water source and you have discovered a hot place to pigeon hunt.

Bandtails can also be shot in harvested grainfields, where the hunting is akin to dove shooting. Best fields to hunt are often

Photos by Jim Zumbo

The bandtail is similar in size to the barnyard pigeon, 14 inches long and weighing nine to 12 ounces. Bandtails have narrow white bands on the backs of their necks, and gray bands across their long, squared tail feathers.

located near wooded ranges known to harbor good concentrations of pigeons. Scout the field as you would for doves, patterning pigeon flights if possible. Take a stand early in the morning and prior to the afternoon feeding. If your patterning is successful, you might also discover strategic points between grainfields, waterholes and roosts where you can take a stand and pass-shoot pigeons trading back and forth.

Bandtails are tough. For most hunting conditions, use high-brass 6s and 7½s and vary your choke tubes between improved cylinder, modified and full to coincide with the flight range of the pigeons.

Whether hunting in coastal mountains or high-desert woodlands, bandtails can be difficult to find after the shot. A Lab or golden retriever, or one of the versatile gundog breeds, will prove a fine companion and a great help for locating every pigeon you shoot.

Where to Go

The Pacific Coast and southwestern states are the only places in North America to hunt this intriguing game bird. Check regulations carefully for open seasons in these states.

Part III
The Complete Upland Bird Hunter

Photo by Karen Lollo

CHAPTER 14

GAME BIRD CARE AND COOKING

Photo by Joe Workosky

Many areas offer excellent opportunities to bag small game species like rabbits and squirrels while hunting upland birds. These game animals will make a welcome addition to the day's bag.

Having spent a glorious afternoon walking the crisp and painted autumn uplands, thrilling to the whirring of wings, enjoying a variety of challenging shooting, you are blessed with an added treat. The birds you bring home will provide you and your family with a delicious, wholesome dinner. This is true regardless of species, as all upland game birds rate from good to excellent on the table if they are properly cared for and cooked to perfection.

209

Photo by *Michael Hanback*

Even the meat of "gamey" birds like sage grouse tastes delicious when properly cared for and cooked to perfection.

This chapter, featuring field-dressing techniques and a selection of recipes, will help you achieve culinary delight from your bounty of upland birds.

Cleaning Birds

The following field-dressing techniques apply to all upland game birds, from tiny quail to six-pound sage grouse. The only tools you need are a sharp pocketknife or bird knife, bottle of water, paper towels and plastic bags.

To prevent meat from tainting and to enhance its flavor, all birds should be gutted or field dressed as quickly as possible after they hit the ground. This is especially important when hunting early in the season, or whenever shooting in warm weather.

To field dress a game bird, make a small horizontal cut near the bird's anus. Then simply reach into the body cavity and remove all the innards with your fingers. At this point you may wish to save the gizzard, heart and liver; these can be cleaned and used to make excellent giblet gravy.

After field dressing the bird, you may continue cleaning it in the field, or slip it into your vest and finish up upon returning

Photo by Michael Hanback

To keep meat from tainting, many hunters draw birds as soon as they hit the ground. This is especially important when hunting in warm weather.

home. One word of caution if finishing afield. You must be able to identify migratory doves and woodcock to a conservation officer if he checks your license and game bag. For this reason, leave a feathered wing (or head) on all migratory birds. Transporting them without attached proof of identity can be a federal offense.

An upland bird can be plucked or skinned. The choice should be determined by the method of cooking or specific recipe you intend to use.

Plucking, in which you begin wherever you wish on the bird's body and remove all feathers by pulling with the grain, takes time. Plucking, however, leaves the skin on the bird. The skin retains juices when cooking, helping to keep meat moist.

Skinning is simpler. You merely pull feathers, skin and all from the bird's body. Many upland recipes specify skinless whole birds or parts.

Once gutted and plucked or skinned, the bird's head is easily removed with your knife. Some hunters save the neck and add it to their giblet gravy. At this time the bird's crop, the small neck pouch that stores seeds and grain in the first steps of digestion, should be removed. Simply pull off the crop or use your knife to remove it. As an aid to future hunts, cut open the crop and

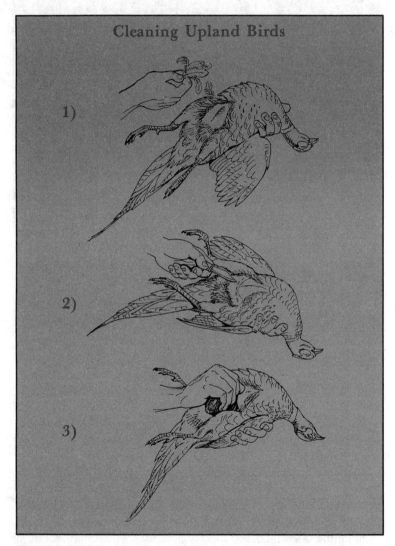

Cleaning Upland Birds

1)

2)

3)

Proper handling of bagged upland birds saves time and ensures best quality meat. 1) Most hunters field dress upland birds soon after shooting. Pluck belly feathers. 2) Open the body from breast bone to anus. 3) Insert fingers and remove entrails; drain and cool body cavity. The bird is now ready for plucking or skinning.

Photo by Charles J. Farmer

When handled and prepared properly, wild game birds are flavorful and high in nutrition.

examine what the bird has been eating. It can tip you off as to which feeding areas to hunt next time out.

Take off the bird's legs and feet. Cut at the middle joint, leaving tiny (on quail) to medium-sized (on the biggest grouse) drumsticks.

When recipes call for it, you may wish to breast birds. This is simple and easy to do. First pluck or skin the breast, then fillet the meat from the breastbone with your knife. Cut deeply, slowly and carefully, taking pains to save every edible sliver of meat. With some birds, doves in particular, you can insert your fingers into the soft spot below the rear portion of the breastbone and pull upward, freeing the entire breastbone with meat intact.

Next, thoroughly wash all whole birds and breasts in cold water. With tweezers or the sharp point of a knife remove as many shot pellets as possible. If you plan to eat the birds soon, storing them in the refrigerator for a few days can enhance their flavor.

To freeze upland birds, place them in plastic freezer bags or cling wrap, press out all air, wrap tightly in heavy freezer paper and tape and seal securely. Many hunters freeze their birds in water, believing this protects them from drying out and burning in the freezer. Simply choose a plastic freezer bag large enough for the birds, fill with water and freeze solid.

Recipes

Photo by Charles J. Farmer

Whether you will be grilling dove breasts on the barbecue, roasting quail or baking sage grouse in marinade, you will find a wide array of recipes in game cookbooks today. From these cookbooks, select several recipes that strike your fancy and perfect them. Don't be afraid to experiment with new techniques and recipes — putting spice and variety into your cooking makes the most of your upland bounty.

To get you started preparing sumptuous game bird meals, try the following recipes from fellow NRA members across North America. These recipes have been tested and given "four star" ratings by expert game cooks. They are featured, along with hundreds more, in the NRA Hunter Services Division's *NRA Members' Wild Game Cookbook*.

Grilled or Broiled Dove

doves
sliced pineapple
jalapeño peppers
thick sliced bacon
pepper
garlic powder, optional
toothpicks

Pluck doves and use game shears to split up the back. Place one inch of pineapple in body cavity along with one half jalapeño pepper. Wrap bacon around dove and secure with a toothpick, then pepper. Cook on outdoor grill or broil indoors. Cook until bacon is crisp and doves are dark brown. Turn at least once to cook each side. Cooking time is about 20 to 30 minutes, total. Figure three doves per person. Serve with Spanish rice and field peas for a crowd pleaser.

Roast Quail

4 whole quail with skin
2 tablespoons butter
1 tablespoon Kitchen Bouquet
your favorite stuffing

Add stuffing to cavities of quail and place them breast side down in a roasting pan. Turn legs toward inside of pan so they don't cook too fast. Mix melted butter and Kitchen Bouquet, brush half mixture on quail. Cover with wax paper and microwave on high for 12 minutes. Turn birds over. Brush on rest of sauce. Microwave another 12 minutes until legs move freely; this is a way to check for doneness. Watch legs and wings carefully and shield with pieces of microwavable wax paper if they start to dry out.

Partridge with Pistachios

4 skinned and boned upland bird breasts quartered
¼ cup shelled unsalted pistachios
¼ teaspoon lemon rind, grated
cracker meal
4 tablespoons butter
1 egg blended with 1 tablespoon water
salt and white pepper to taste
fresh chopped parsley for garnish

Mix salt and white pepper with cracker meal. Dip breasts in egg, then coat with seasoned cracker meal. Melt butter over low heat, sauté pistachios and lemon rind for two minutes. Add breasts to pan and sauté approximately three minutes per side until lightly browned. Place breasts on a platter, sprinkle with pistachios, drizzle butter from pan over top and sprinkle with chopped parsley.

Grouse Bake

4 breasted grouse, soaked overnight in salt water
½ stick of butter
1 teaspoon of salt
½ teaspoon of pepper
⅓ cup of Italian dressing
½ cup of Holland House Tom Collins drink mixer

Pre-heat oven 450 degrees. Arrange birds in a casserole dish. Blend above ingredients and baste birds. Cover and bake 50 to 60 minutes or until done, basting often. Serve with white or wild rice.

Pheasant Gravy with Mushrooms over Toast

1 pheasant, cleaned
¼ cup mushrooms, sliced
1 (10½ ounce) can of condensed cream mushroom soup
1 (10½ ounce) can of condensed cream of chicken soup
½ cup of milk
½ cup of water
toast

Cook pheasant in pot of water, covered, until meat is tender, about one to one and a half hours. Remove pheasant from pot to cool, then de-bone meat and set aside. Sauté mushrooms in a little butter, put pheasant meat and mushrooms in a two and a half quart covered saucepan. Add in both cans of soup, milk and water. Stir and cook over low heat. Add salt and pepper to taste. Serve over toast.

A Bird for the Taxidermist

Having hunted a favorite species of upland game for years, you may finally decide to mount a cock bird. Upon returning from a cross-country hunt, you may bring with you several "exotic" birds for the taxidermist. Perhaps you wish to preserve your son's or daughter's first quail, pheasant or grouse.

A skilled taxidermist can perform excellent, realistic work, but he is no magician. Give him a good bird to work with. This begins by selecting a lightly hit bird, one killed by a few pellets. Feathers should be immaculately intact, and its neck and wings should not be broken.

Photo by Michael Hanback

If you wish to mount an upland bird, give a taxidermist a good specimen to work with. Select a lightly hit bird with feathers, neck and wings intact, and carry your trophy carefully from the field.

Along these lines, beat your dog to the retrieve if you desire a bird for preservation. A saliva-soaked bird with teeth marks can cause trouble for a taxidermist.

Carry the bird carefully from the field. If you must walk far, tuck its head beneath a wing (to protect the neck from breaking) and wrap it lightly in brown paper. Also, stuff a gun-cleaning patch or ball of cotton inside the bird's mouth. This keeps blood and other fluids from seeping out of the bird's bill onto the feathers.

In warm weather, never carry a bird in a plastic bag; it will spoil quickly. Some hunters carry a woman's nylon stocking afield and "hose" the bird, pulling the stocking over the bird's body head first. The stocking "breathes" and protects the bird in transit. If you cannot get your bird to a taxidermist immediately, freeze it solid.

Handle your bird carefully, and chances are it will turn out a realistic, beautiful mount that rekindles fond hunting memories for years to come.

Photo by Joe Workosky

Photographs of your favorite hunts will be invaluable to you in years to come. Good 35mm camera gear helps capture those special moments.

CHAPTER 15

BIRD HUNTING SAFETY AND ETHICS

Photo by Leonard Lee Rue III

Handling and pointing your shotgun carefully, positively identifying legal game birds and shooting only in clear, safe zones are but a few of the many safety factors you must consider every time you step afield.

Upland bird hunting, like all forms of hunting, is inherently a safe sport. While millions of wingshooters take to the fields each autumn, relatively few accidents occur. Thanks in large part to the excellent hunter education and safety efforts of the past decade, upland bird hunting has become one of the safest forms of outdoor recreation in North America today.

Wingshooters, novice or expert, must remember that each time they step afield, one careless, overzealous moment can, in a split-second, turn a fine day of bird hunting into a tragedy. Indeed, all hunters must keep firearms and field safety firmly and foremost in mind.

Firearms Safety

While the following safety creeds apply to all hunting situations in which a firearm is involved, they have been listed here with the upland bird hunter in mind.

1. Always control your shotgun's muzzle and point it in a safe direction.

2. Be absolutely positive of your target (bird) before shooting.

Photo by Michael Hanback

Never mix shotshells. Check your gunning vest before each hunt, making sure to carry only the proper loads for your shotgun. This is especially important if you regularly switch between a 12- and 20-gauge.

3. Take time to fire safely. If in a rush and unsure if your shotgun is properly mounted, pass up the shot. If there is any doubt whatsoever whether to shoot, don't.

4. Use the proper ammunition for your shotgun. Never mix different types of shotshells. If hunting with a 12-gauge, never carry 20-gauge shells in your pockets or gunning vest.

5. If you slip while walking, control the shotgun's muzzle and point it in a safe direction. After a fall, unload the gun and check carefully for barrel obstructions such as dirt, mud and snow.

6. Always unload your shotgun before traversing hazardous terrain, such as a steep bank, deep ditch or icy creek.

7. When hunting alone and crossing a fence, unload your shotgun and place it under the fence, with the muzzle pointed safely away from your body at all times. Take this into consideration on both sides of the fence. When hunting with partners, unload your gun, open its action and have a companion hold the gun while you cross the fence. Then hold your partners' unloaded shotguns while they cross safely.

8. Maintain your firearm wisely. Always keep it clean. Never use a shotgun that is in poor condition, malfunctioning or incapable of handling safely the shotshells you use.

9. Be aware of the range of your loads. Before shooting make certain shot pellets cannot rain down on other hunters in the area.

10. Adverse weather conditions, fatigue and the excitement of hunting can impair your physical and mental performance afield. Rain, wind and snow can inhibit your concentration on firearms safety. Rainwear, or heavy winter clothing, can cause poor shotgun handling and mounting. Fatigue can cause carelessness and clumsiness. Excitement, such as a game bird flushing wildly underfoot, can cause overzealousness. For maximum safety, monitor and control these conditions as closely as possible.

11. At all times be aware of your shotgun's safety. Remember to place it back on (double-check this frequently afield) after each bird shooting opportunity has passed.

12. Establish safe zones of fire when hunting with companions. Be sure your shotgun's muzzle is always pointed safely in your zone. Never fire at a flushing bird that crosses into another hunter's zone, or whips back between the two of you.

13. Alcohol and drugs, which impair your judgement and reflexes, obviously don't mix with firearms and hunting.

14. After each day's hunt, unload your shotgun in the field

Photo by Wicker Bill

NRA Staff Photo

When bird hunting with partner, "zones of fire" must be established so each hunter won't endanger the others. Remember, upland bird hunting requires that you follow all rules for safe gun handling, such as opening your action and setting your gun down before crossing a fence, or handing it to another hunter.

and keep its action open. Never enter a vehicle, camp or house with a loaded shotgun.

15. If companions violate any of these rules of safe firearms handling, bring it to their attention at once. Refuse to hunt with anyone who refuses to correct his or her behavior and continues to handle firearms carelessly afield.

Photos by Joe Workosky

When hunting in cold, snowy weather, your extra clothing should allow safe gun handling and mounting. Also, make certain snow never plugs your shotgun barrel.

Bird Hunting Safety

Safety Orange

Most upland gunners, dove hunters excluded, should wear at least a safety-orange cap. An orange vest or coat provides maximum visibility in thick bird cover. As mentioned earlier in this book, many state laws require bird hunters to wear a certain amount of orange clothing.

For upland hunters, fluorescent orange offers two important safety advantages:

- Easily seen at great distances, it allows you and your partners to keep track of each other as you fan out parallel across a cover.
- A hunter in orange is instantaneously visible to another shooter swinging on quick-flushing and crossing birds.

223

Photo by Michael Hanback

Briers and brambles can easily obstruct your view of another hunter. Wear at least an orange cap and keep close track of partners when fanning out across thick bird cover. If in doubt of another hunter's exact location, never shoot.

Safety Afield

In addition to proper shotgun handling, consider the following field safety tips.

- Since upland bird hunters typically hike a lot, careful walking is essential. A slow, methodical walk across a bird cover is better than fast-paced racing. In addition to being more effective at finding and flushing birds, a safe, comfortable pace protects your knees and ankles. Fast, haphazard walking over unlevel ground can lead to sprained knees and turned or broken ankles. While this will obviously ruin your day when hunting close to home, it can be a serious problem when hunting miles deep into remote country. So slow down for maximum safety.

Photo by Stan Kirkland, Florida Game and Fresh Water Fish Commission

Slow, methodical, watch-your-step walking is better than fast-paced sprinting. You'll keep from turning an ankle and find more birds.

- Much bird hunting around the country, especially early in the season, is conducted in warm to hot weather. If not careful an upland hunter, sweating profusely beneath a blazing sun, can dehydrate quickly. Be sure to carry an ample supply of water and wear a brimmed hat afield. Take frequent breaks in the shade, especially if you feel light-headed and dizzy. Be on the lookout for the effects of sun-induced exhaustion or heat stroke.

225

- Always wear shooting glasses.
- Carry map, compass and first-aid gear in remote country.
- Remember that planning hunts wisely and using common sense afield are the best medicines for preventing problems.

These are, of course, only several factors to keep in mind. Combine them with other safety tips scattered throughout this book to devise a field safety checklist that suits your personal style of bird hunting.

Bird Hunting Ethics

Ethics encompasses the many responsibilities an upland bird hunter has to other hunters, landowners, the general public and the game. Through hunting laws and regulations, federal, state and provincial governments require certain standards of ethical behavior. In many cases, however, it is up to the individual to decide what is right and what is wrong, and then hunt according to his or her personal standards.

Some ethical questions are simple; others are complex. Most matters of ethics can be resolved by answering the following question: Is this pursuit legal and fair to all parties concerned, including the game birds and myself? The following standards you may follow, but ultimately you must decide.

Responsibilities to Other Hunters

Besides safety, you have several responsibilities to fellow hunters. First, if you find another person in the cover where you planned to bird hunt, leave the area. Moving in on another hunter is not only discourteous, but can be extremely unsafe. Respect the rights of fellow bird hunters — hopefully one day you will be on the receiving end of ethical hunting.

Without being rude, attempt to pass on responsible behavior to all fellow bird hunters. If a partner refuses to hunt responsibly, cease hunting with him or her.

Don't litter, drive vehicles or otherwise disturb an area where others are hunting. Most bird hunters have deep personal feelings for nature and the environment, and find great peace of mind while hunting. Don't violate them.

Responsibilities to Landowners

Each year, thousands of acres of private land are posted "No

Photo by James M. Norine

Always obtain permission before bird hunting on private property. Hunt safely and ethically, and a landowner will welcome you back season after season.

Hunting" because unethical hunters treated the land or its owner with disrespect. This severely hurts all hunters.

Always obtain permission before bird hunting on private property. Approach a landowner courteously, not only because it enhances your chances of getting permission, but also because it promotes a positive image of the hunter. Having obtained permission to bird hunt, treat the land with utmost care. Leave no signs you were there. Take litter and spent shotshells with you each day as you leave. Never drive your vehicle on soft, muddy ground.

To keep good landowner relations intact, avoid disturbing livestock, fences, croplands and other property. Leave all gates as they were found—either opened or closed. Don't abuse your welcome by overhunting the area or bringing a carload of companions.

Finally, a small token of your appreciation—a card, gift or offer to help around the farm or ranch at harvest time—will go a long way toward keeping your permission to bird hunt year after year.

Responsibilities to the Public

Remember that the environment and upland game birds belong

to everyone, not just hunters. Respect the rights of people who enjoy nature without hunting. Avoid shooting in areas where you know non-hunters are experiencing the outdoors. Keep spent shell cases and other signs of hunting out of view. Don't display bagged birds to people who may not want to see them. Don't clean your birds in plain view of the public. In short, remember that in some cases unfavorable public opinion has resulted in restrictive hunting laws and regulations.

The upland bird hunter owes it to the public to enforce all hunting laws. The upland gunner must abide by all laws and report those who trespass, poach or vandalize property.

Responsibilities to the Game

Upland birds, like all game, deserve the utmost respect of hunters. A wingshooter who does not revel in the excitement of the chase, who fails to feel a special reverence for delicately beautiful doves, quail, pheasants, woodcock or grouse, is missing the very essence of bird hunting.

You must strive to kill birds cleanly. Never fire indiscriminately into a flock, or take any shot that has a strong chance of crippling. Then you must make every possible effort to find downed birds. And of course you must never exceed bag limits or resort to illegal or unsportsmanlike methods to fill a limit.

Do your part in the conservation and promotion of upland birds. In doing so, you are also conserving and promoting the future of upland bird hunting. One way to get involved is to join organizations such as Pheasants Forever, Inc., Quail Unlimited, Inc., or The Ruffed Grouse Society.

A responsible bird hunter should make every effort to learn as much about his quarry as possible. The National Rifle Association of America conducts clinics, provides members with hunting information, and offers other benefits to hunters and gun owners.

Responsibilities to Yourself

Finally, don't forget responsibilities to yourself. If a certain bird hunting law or regulation conflicts with your carefully considered ethical beliefs, work to change the law. Fight it with letters and votes, not disobedience. Don't take a chance and violate your ethics in any way. You will regret it later.

In the end, hunt hard and honestly. You will have fun and be proud of your sportsmanship.

Photo by Charles J. Farmer

Photo by Nick Hromiak

You have a responsibility to the gamebirds you hunt. This includes, when available, taking a well-trained gundog along as your hunting partner.

229

Photo by Michael Hanback

Take only good shots, striving to kill all birds quickly and cleanly. You'll feel reverence for the delicately beautiful uplanders you hold in hand.

Pass Along the Tradition

If you are a dedicated upland bird hunter, you will, over the days, weeks, seasons and years, develop a deep concern for the future of your glorious sport. Ultimately you will reach the point where you derive the most pleasure and satisfaction from introducing others, particularly youngsters, to the fine pursuit of upland birds.

Instruct new hunters early on safety, ethics and responsibility because their respect and appreciation of our hunting heritage will determine the future of hunting.

Photo by Joe Workosky

Photo by Joe Workosky   *Photo by Charles J. Farmer*

Youngsters are the future of upland bird hunting. Teach them to hunt hard, safely and ethically, and the splendid sport will be in good hands.

Appendix

Photo by Joe Workosky

THE NRA AND HUNTING

The National Rifle Association of America encourages and supports sport hunting through a wide variety of programs and services.

The NRA Hunter Services Division assists state and provincial hunter education programs with support materials and training programs for professional and volunteer staff. NRA Hunter Clinics, offered by an NRA sponsored event or a trained instructor, answer the demand for advanced education by emphasizing skills, responsibility, and safety as applied to hunting techniques and game species. The NRA Youth Hunter Education Challenge uses hunting simulated events to give young hunters a chance to apply basic skills learned in the classroom on local, state and national level. Financial support for wildlife management and shooting sports research is available through the NRA Grants-in-Aid Program.

The NRA Institute for Legislative Action protects the legal rights of hunters. NRA Publications provides a variety of printed material on firearms, equipment and techniques for hunters, including *American Hunter* magazine, the largest periodical in the U. S. devoted to hunting. Junior programs encourage young people to participate in hunting. Special insurance benefits are available to NRA hunting members, and hunters can further benefit by joining an NRA hunting club or by affiliating an existing club with the NRA. The NRA works with other hunting organizations to sustain a positive image of hunting as a traditional form of recreation, to combat anti-hunting efforts, and to promote a life-long interest in hunting.

For further information, contact the National Rifle Association of America, Hunter Services Division, 1600 Rhode Island Avenue, N.W., Washington, D.C. 20036–3268. Telephone (202) 828–6259.

To join NRA today, or for additional information regarding membership, please call 1–800–368–5714. Your membership dues can be charged to VISA or MasterCard.

NRA MATERIALS FOR THE UPLAND BIRD HUNTER

The following are available from the NRA Sales Department and can help you prepare for your next upland bird trip.

Description	Item No.	Unit Price
The Hunter's Guide	HE5N5090	$ 8.95 each
NRA Hunter Skills Series		
Student's Manual		
Upland Bird Hunting	HS5N5476	$ 5.00 each
Bowhunting	HS5N5403	$ 5.00 each
Muzzleloader Hunting	HS5N5145	$ 5.00 each
Whitetail Deer Hunting	HS5N5305	$ 5.00 each
Western Big Game Hunting	HS5N5207	$ 5.00 each
Waterfowl Hunting	HS5N5083	$ 5.00 each
Wild Turkey Hunting	HS5N5707	$ 5.00 each
Hardbound Version		
Upland Bird Hunting	HS5N5501	$14.95 each
Bowhunting	HS5N5449	$14.95 each
Muzzleloader Hunting	HS5N5172	$14.95 each
Whitetail Deer Hunting	HS5N5261	$14.95 each
Western Big Game Hunting	HS5N5243	$14.95 each
Waterfowl Hunting	HS5N5136	$14.95 each
Wild Turkey Hunting	HS5N5734	$14.95 each
NRA Members' Wild Game Cookbook	HS5N5805	$12.95 each
Life-Size Game Targets*		
Brochure	HS3N0017	N/C
Pheasant Set of 5	HS5N1247	$ 4.00
Pheasant Set of 50	HS5N1363	$35.00
Package containing one each:		
Whitetail Deer, Turkey,		
Duck, Rabbit, Groundhog,		
Mule Deer Black Bear,		
Pronghorn, Javelina,		
Coyote, Red Fox, Pheasant,		
and Squirrel	HS5N1023	$10.00

*Note: Various package quantities are available.

NRA Hunter Clinic Program
Brochure — Keeping the
Tradition Alive and Flourishing! HS3N0053   N/C
NRA Hunter Clinic Instructor
Certification Order Form   HS3N8037   N/C

Other Brochures
Wild Game From Field to Table HI3N0080   N/C
Hunting and Wildlife
Management   HE3N0140   N/C
Landowner Relations   HE3N0033   N/C
Responsible Hunting   HE3N0024   N/C
Hypothermia   HE3N0079   N/C
Fitness and Nutrition   HE3N0097   N/C
Water Safety   HE3N0051   N/C
Tree Stand Safety   HE3N0015   N/C
Turkey Hunting Safety   HE3N0113   N/C
Hunting's Future? It's Up to You HE3N0104   N/C
Eye and Ear Care   HE3N0042   N/C
The NRA and Hunting   HI3N0115   N/C

NRA Hunter Services Division
Materials Price List   HI3N8091   N/C

NRA Standard Order Form   XS7N8000   N/C

ORDERING INFORMATION

- Use the NRA Standard Order Form to order items listed. Prices are subject to change without notice.
- Prices do not include shipping and handling charges. Certain state sales taxes are applicable.
- Order forms and current prices are available from NRA Sales Department, P.O. Box 5000, Kearneysville, WV 25430-5000 or call **toll free 1-800-336-7402**. Hours: 9:00 a.m. to 5:00 p.m. Eastern time, weekdays only.

FUTURE NRA MATERIALS
FOR THE UPLAND BIRD HUNTER

Other items for the upland bird hunter soon to be available from the NRA Sales Department:
NRA Hunter Skills Series — Upland Bird Hunting
Instructor's Manual
NRA Hunter Clinic Safety Orange Cap (Winter)

THE NRA HUNTER SKILLS SERIES

T he NRA Hunter Skills Series is a developing library of books on hunting, shooting, and related activities. It supports the NRA Hunter Clinic Program, a national network of seminars conducted by the NRA Hunter Services Division and volunteer hunter clinic instructors.

The hunter training manuals are developed by NRA staff, with the assistance of noted hunting experts, hunter educators, experienced outdoor writers, and representatives of hunting/conservation organizations. The publications are available in student (bound) and instructor (loose leaf) editions.

The program is planned to include clinics and support material on hunting whitetail deer, waterfowl, wild turkey, small game, predators, upland game, western big game, and others. It will also address marksmanship and hunting with rifle, shotgun, muzzleloader, handgun, and archery equipment.

For more information about the NRA Hunter Clinic Program and its training materials, contact National Rifle Association of America, Hunter Services Division, 1600 Rhode Island Avenue, N.W., Washington, D.C. 20036-3268. Telephone (202) 828-6259.